ART   IDEAS   HISTORY

THE STRUCTURES
OF THE
MODERN WORLD

1850-1900

NELLO PONENTE

TRANSLATED FROM THE ITALIAN BY JAMES EMMONS

★

Distributed in the United States by
THE WORLD PUBLISHING COMPANY
2231 West 110th Street, Cleveland 2, Ohio

★

★

PRINTED IN SWITZERLAND

CONTENTS

I

THE TASTE OF A PERIOD

II

A NEW ORDER

III

THE DIMENSION OF THE MIND

HONORÉ DAUMIER (1808-1879). RATAPOIL, 1850. BRONZE. LOUVRE, PARIS.

I

THE TASTE OF A PERIOD

THE PROUD CENTURY

The period was full of contrasts: progressing rapidly in some directions, it lagged behind in others. It was the "proud century that thought itself secure against the misfortunes of Greece and Rome," as Baudelaire described it in writing of the Paris World's Fair of 1855. It was the century of imperialism. But for all its pride it was prone to temporizing, misgivings, philistinism; it longed for a return to the past as a way of escape from the drab materialism of the present and the responsibilities pressing upon it from all sides. The period began with the failure of all the hopes kindled by the Revolution of 1848. It arose on the unsteady foundations laid by the initial phase of the Industrial Revolution, in progress for a century past. It came to a close in an era whose self-assurance and optimism are seen today to have been wholly unjustified. It ended with a hymn to progress—progress which certainly yielded great results on the material plane but which seems to have been unsustained by any solid moral basis. The *belle époque* was by no means so delightful as it has been made out to be by the myth-makers who have seized upon it.

By the middle of the century the liberal, democratic spirit of 1848 had failed to achieve its aims. The Communist Manifesto published by Marx gave the new classes high hopes for the future—but that future was remote. Middle-class democracy took the form of paternalism in France; elsewhere on the continent it was rejected like a heresy. The growing power of capitalism in England, which led the way in industrialization, was still a blind force for which no one had yet found the laws and regulations that might harness it. The traditional urban landscape was transformed, city and country underwent radical changes, but with rare exceptions there was no general awareness of the necessity for town planning.

The analysis of conditions among the working class in England published by Engels in 1845 was a social denunciation that went far beyond the simple description of the evils afflicting one particular class; it indicted a whole society incapable of coming to grips not only with social problems but with the slums and squalor of city life which were the root cause of those social conditions. "Below the bridge you look upon the piles of débris, the refuse, filth, and offal from the courts on the steep left bank; here each house is packed close behind its neighbor and a piece of each is visible, all black, smoky, crumbling, ancient, with broken panes and window frames. The background is furnished by old barrack-like factory buildings." Such was one quarter of Manchester, as Engels saw it. A writer no less than a sociologist could not but be appalled at the drabness, the physical and moral degradation of the new industrial centers: the Coketown described by Dickens in *Hard Times* in 1854 is the nineteenth-century counterpart of the "red desert" denounced by Antonioni in 1964.

The new structures of society emerged very slowly, and not without profound contradictions. Urban development offered great opportunities for building speculators and helped to determine the monotonous uniformity of the townscape. Yet this period also saw the realization of some great town-planning schemes, and there was now for the first time a definite awareness of the problems raised by the growth of cities. But the whole spirit of the age was full of these contradictions, conflicts, and collisions between individual cognizance and collective cognizance. This was the period of the first great engineering projects, but also of the conflict which in France opposed the Ecole des Beaux-Arts to the Ecole Polytechnique. This was the century that raised the banner of scientific progress, but it was also that of the Syllabus of Pius IX. The world of the spirit strove to distinguish itself from the world of technology, for it rightly feared that the latter, as it came to create a social system in its own image, would tend to reduce the part played by other activities, by art in particular.

Ruskin stigmatized this trend and so did William Morris—all his ideas and ventures were conceived in reaction against it. But this problem, particularly where the acute social sensibility of artists and intellectuals was concerned, remained a personal one and each had to solve it for himself as best he could. It was solved by the great engineers and architects, from Eiffel to Sullivan, who employed the materials provided by new techniques and in doing so discovered new means of expression in no way inferior to those of the much-admired past. It was solved by those who, breaking away from eclecticism and throwing off the fetters of convention, realized that there is no real conflict between expression and technique, and that therefore the language of artistic communication is not to be identified with a canon of beauty, but with an ideology. Gone were the days when people dilated on the "beautiful" and the "sublime." The discussion centered now on the identity between intention and execution which went to determine a new scale of values. That the public should have heaped ridicule on impressionist paintings is understandable, though hardly justified, for the Impressionists were searching for, and found, new values that necessarily called for a different standard of judgment and a new state of mind capable of assimilating them.

The conflict, as we have said, remained a personal one, for it was deeply rooted in the individual psyche and the basic reason for it lay in the fact that the consciousness of each individual was inescapably confronted with a growing body of technical and scientific knowledge with which it had to come to terms. Herein lies the great significance of all the developments, not only technical and artistic but institutional and political, of the second half of the nineteenth century. Wherever the division of knowledge widened the distance between disciplines, infrastructures (rather than structures) were created which, in lingering on, have added to the evils of the twentieth century. As Siegfried Giedion has acutely observed: "If our culture should be destroyed by brutal forces—or even if it should continue to be terrorized by them—then the nineteenth century will have to be judged as having misused men, materials and human thought, as one of the most wretched of periods. If we prove capable of putting to their right use the potentialities which were handed down to us, then the nineteenth century, in spite of the human disorder it created

and in spite of the consequences which are still developing out of it, will grow into new and heroic dimensions."

For the nineteenth century had its great men, even though it used them ill, and it had them in an abundance which has fortunately continued down to our time. It was these men who created not only the structures of our society but the structures of our sensibility. Today it is easy to deride the taste and pretensions of that time, easy to condemn its obstinate rejection of every innovation, its tame acceptance of the products of the stalest conventionalism. But the period that began with David and ended with Cézanne saw a quick succession of revolutions, a remolding of habits and relationships, and a tremendous increase in the speed of communications, from the gallop of a horse to the complete abolition of distance by means of wireless telegraphy, invented by Marconi in 1895.

The potentialities of the century were therefore enormous, so great that the keenest minds, already foreseeing the consequences, were seriously alarmed. Peter Viereck, in an essay entitled *The Muse and the Machine*, has recently called attention to a remark of Goethe's in the third book of *Wilhelm Meisters Wanderjahre*: "This rapid spread of machinery troubles and frightens me. It is gathering like a storm, slowly, slowly; but it is moving towards us, and it will come and burst upon us." *Wilhelm Meisters Wanderjahre* appeared in its final form in 1829. The ineluctable process of mechanization aroused fears of what, a century later, Ortega y Gasset was to call the dehumanization of art. It filled Dickens with dismay, it led Ruskin and Morris to invoke the freedom of the medieval arts and crafts: all feared to see what they held to be the peculiar qualities of the mind overwhelmed and crushed by matter. The century witnessed an ever-widening cleavage between art and science, and its leading personalities set themselves the task of reconciling and reuniting them, in so far as possible, through a reappraisal of the traditional ideologies—a task in which they were only partially successful, for in many respects that cleavage still exists.

Not many years however after the publication of *Wilhelm Meisters Wanderjahre*, another poet took a more sanguine view of the future than Goethe. In 1850 Théophile Gautier wrote: "Mankind must create a totally new architecture, born of today, now that use is being made of new systems created by the industry that is just coming into existence. The application of cast-iron allows and demands the use of many new forms, such as can be seen in railway stations, in suspension bridges, in the arches of greenhouses." The "faultless poet," the "perfect magician of French literature," the admirer of Ingres and pure beauty, the theorist of art for art's sake, Gautier was discerning enough to realize that the new materials and techniques called for new forms, that a cast-iron column could not simply imitate a Greek column, above all that the new materials had a nobility of their own in no way inferior to that of traditional materials. The new architecture could not be confined to bridges or greenhouses, like the one built by Rouhault in 1833 for the Jardin des Plantes in Paris. Gautier's comments reveal the keen critical perceptions which enabled him in 1861, in spite of his prejudices, to divine the greatness of Manet when he saw the *Guitar Player* at the Salon of that year: "There is a great deal of talent in this life-sized figure, painted in heavy impasto, with a spirited brush and in colors that ring true." But the few decades that separated Goethe from Gautier had not only revolutionized industrial processes, they had also raised the problem of a new sensibility, untrammeled by the academicism which was now a dead weight in the art world, corresponding to none of the realities of the new age.

But it was no easy matter to enter into this new sensibility and Gautier himself had been aware of this earlier, in 1857, when in speaking of Delacroix he recorded proudly that he "had foreseen, before most people, all that genius implies in the way of future achievement." For in fact the century also took pride in its ability to single out the creative moments of the new age, at a time when the current sensibility was intensely hostile to any innovation. For most people art could only be a means of escape, a longed-for return to the past, or an outright glorification of political conservatism. The new working classes, now beginning to be conscious of their condition and to struggle against the rigidity of the social structure, had neither the leisure nor the ability to keep abreast of events in the art world. It was all they could do to keep body and soul together. Escape thus meant for the ruling class a rejection of whatever new knowledge art could provide. Taine gave warning that to under-stand an artist or group of artists, the spirit and customs of the age they lived in must first be understood; for Proudhon art had to fulfill a social purpose. These were great truths, though they may then have seemed great illusions. Not only at that time was there a cleavage between technology and politics, as we have seen; there was an even greater one between art, technology and politics. The paternalism of the Second Empire would not and could not recognize any social import in Manet's works; and though it allowed Haussmann to change the face of Paris and accepted Labrouste's designs for the Bibliothèque Sainte-Geneviève and the Bibliothèque Nationale, it did so without realizing the full implications of these steps.

More prudent and astute, English conservatism adjusted itself more easily to innovations, though it must be admitted that the English painters of that day did not raise comparable problems. England, however, passed the first laws dealing with town planning and it had men like Sir Henry Cole who, even before Morris, was concerned about the relationship between industrial and artistic production. The great democracy across the ocean which was going through a crisis of its own, arising out of the conflict between the industrialized North and the agrarian and conservative South, was also trying to find its bearings. No more of the architecture of President Jefferson who sought to hark back ideally to the republican institutions of Greece and Rome, no more of the eighteenth-century rationalism of L'Enfant's plan of Washington: it was time now for a fresh consideration of materials and structures. Bogardus used supporting columns of iron, Richardson rejected European Neoclassicism and Neo-Gothic, and Horatio Greenough, an academic sculptor, actively campaigned for a new architecture and proclaimed that "form follows function." The United States thus achieved a style of architectural design in perfect keeping with the historical development of the young nation; this was especially true after the rise of the Chicago School and the achievements of Louis Sullivan, the outstanding architectural designer of the nineteenth century.

But not even the young and apparently most progressive nations are proof against reactionary temptations. The World's Columbian Exposition held at Chicago in 1893 saw the downfall of the ideals of the great American architects; it seemed deliberately designed to deepen the cleavage, to disavow the progress so far made, to restore the conditions that Frank Lloyd Wright has singled out as characteristic of the dissension: "Wanton denials of humanity were made by machine-power, abetted by the impotence of artists and architects, themselves blind to the fresh opportunities, really their duties. Such failures as they were making of life, then as now, were a standardized slander upon the liberated individual rather than any true reflection of his innate power. Thus doomed to spiritual sterility, art and architecture were facing extinction in all the hell there was."

The century also took a negative pride in the extent to which others were powerless to affirm their superiority. In France it is clear that Couture, towards the middle of the century, and Bonnat, at the end of it, best represented the tastes of a society that found in them exactly what it wanted: conformity, conventionalism, no questionings or anxieties. For Edmond About, writing of the 1855 World's Fair, Courbet stood condemned because he showed himself to have a "hatred of style." About was a reactionary, but even the progressive-minded could be obtuse on occasion. Zola was moved to break with the Impressionists, to declare his old friend Cézanne to be a failure as an artist. Zola would have liked Cézanne to paint scenes of modern life; yet when Eiffel built the tower that bears his name, Zola signed a letter of protest. In earlier days he had shown a finer grasp of things, not only when he sprang to Manet's defense but when, in *Le Ventre de Paris*, he described certain aspects of the Paris markets with a simplicity and color that bring to mind Manet's still lifes. But by 1886, when he published *L'Œuvre*, Zola appeared unable to understand that the painting of his day had rejected all forms of celebration and was no longer interested in raising monuments. As Lionello Venturi has pointed out (citing the title of a book by Daniel Halévy for his purpose), this art period, that of the Impressionists in particular, brought about "something similar to what has been called in French political life the *fin des notables*: the end of elegance and display, the beginning of a new dignity for the humiliated masses." Yet paternalism was proud of itself, for it thought it represented the optimum and dismissed art as a mere corollary, on an altogether lower plane, of political activity. The great source of incomprehension can be traced to this view of

art, which it was thought could be harnessed in the service of other ends, just as industrial power at the same time was harnessing the craftsman and so condemning him to extinction. As the proletariat became the slave of the machine which, as Morris saw, deprived him of every incentive to personal invention, so the artist had to be bound to the traditional working techniques, which gave no scope for any originality.

In the last analysis, it was the dignity of human labor, of whatever kind, that was not being respected, and whoever laid claim to it was a revolutionary. A few concessions might be made to the worker—as the Salon des Refusés had been granted to artists—as a generous and condescending gift from above. "I hope, Monsieur Courbet," said Count Nieuwerkerke, Imperial Director of Fine Arts, "that you will not have occasion to complain of the benevolence of the Government with regard to yourself; no one can flatter himself on having had so much. Please take note that luncheon is being offered to you today not by me but by the Government." Nor did things change much under the Republic. Rivière tells how Renoir, a friend of Gambetta, appealed to the statesman to get an article published favorable to the impressionist exhibition of 1877; but when he entered the office of one of the editors of a paper called *La République Française*, he was met with the words: "It is out of the question, it would be scandalous. Do you not see that you are revolutionaries?"

To understand the great artistic achievements of the second half of the nineteenth century, we must remember that they flew in the face of the traditional conception of the relation between artist and society. The rejection of the monumental, by all painters, sculptors and architects worthy of the name, was one aspect of the change and amounted in effect to a vindication of the dignity of the artist's handiwork. When the architect made use of new materials, he did not mean to be imposed on by technology; he took them up deliberately and his choice of materials was a critical choice. Monet and Pissarro believed that significant and effective communication could be achieved by simply painting a haystack. No need of proud swelling rhetoric. The lesson of the age, its moral as well as its aesthetic message, have come to form an integral part of the sensibility and endeavor of our own century.

THE VALUE OF THE IMAGE

Realism was a reaction against academic painting. Refusing to idealize the human figure, the Realists depicted men and women in the setting of daily life, going about their daily tasks, and this proved to be a fruitful source of inspiration. Millet sent in to the 1848 Salon a picture (later destroyed by fire in the United States) representing a peasant winnowing grain, the first of a series of pictures of peasant life, one of which is reproduced here. At that time, however, he still attached too much importance to the subject, rather to the detriment of form; in this respect Millet was following in the footsteps of Decamps. Ten years later the pictorial sensibility of Daumier had wrought a profound change: in his Butcher *the figure of the man intent on his work is treated in the same manner as the quartered animal, with a synthesis of line and condensed colors which was not to be lost on Cézanne. A little later, Manet painted his* Street Singer *(1862) and Renoir his* Lise with a Sunshade *(1867). Both have the vigorous and sturdy forms typical of Realism, and in fact Lise herself repeats almost exactly the pose of the central figure of Courbet's* Village Maidens. *These pictures, however, for all their undoubted elegance, were even more distasteful to the public than Millet's peasants; for they dealt a blow at conventions, showed the human figure in natural attitudes, and caught the spirit of modern life in their subtle handling of bright colors and glowing light, which shocked a public accustomed to the cold tones of academic painting.*

To break with convention also meant to make light of myths that had outlived their day. The Bathers *Courbet sent in to the 1853 Salon are irreverent nymphs, concerned not with striking graceful attitudes but with imposing the realistic sensuality of their presence. Napoleon III was taken aback when he saw this canvas at the Salon and in a fit of temper struck at it with his riding whip—proof enough that Courbet had hit the mark, for he equated the revolt against prevailing tastes in art with a revolt against the paternalistic, anti-democratic government of the Second Empire. Manet was not cut out to be a political rebel, but with his painting he wrought a revolution which struck home even more forcibly. His* Déjeuner sur l'herbe, *which created a scandal at the Salon des Refusés in 1863, was even less respectful of tradition. With the subtle atmospheric coloring which distinguishes it, the* Déjeuner *did violence to rooted habits of seeing and the accepted logic of narrative art. The picture of a laborer might be forgivable, but not that of a young woman in the nude seated between two men fully clothed. Bourgeois prudery felt the very ground of its convictions giving way beneath it. No one could foresee that the* Déjeuner sur l'herbe *would mark the first step towards an art newly made to the measure of man.*

JEAN-FRANÇOIS MILLET (1814-1875). THE WINNOWER. LOUVRE, PARIS.

HONORÉ DAUMIER (1808-1879). THE BUTCHER, ABOUT 1857-1858. FOGG ART MUSEUM, HARVARD UNIVERSITY (ALPHEUS HAYTT FUND).

EDOUARD MANET (1832-1883). THE STREET SINGER, 1862. ON LOAN TO THE MUSEUM OF FINE ARTS, BOSTON.

AUGUSTE RENOIR (1841-1919). LISE WITH A SUNSHADE, 1867. FOLKWANG MUSEUM, ESSEN.

GUSTAVE COURBET (1819-1877). BATHERS, 1853. MUSÉE FABRE, MONTPELLIER.

EDOUARD MANET (1832-1883). LE DÉJEUNER SUR L'HERBE, 1863. LOUVRE, PARIS.

THE REJECTION OF AUTHORITY

In his review of the 1847 Salon the critic Théophile Thoré maintained that pictures, like books, should be allowed to come before the public without a royal license. But the time was not yet ripe for freedom and toleration. The authorities had no intention of surrendering their powers of control, and no scruples about using every means of coercion at their disposal: the Imperial Directorate of Fine Arts, the juries that admitted exhibitors and awarded prizes, the teaching staff of the art schools, the conformist press which obeyed orders implicitly.

The so-called Salon des Refusés—a special exhibition, authorized by Napoleon III, of pictures rejected by the jury of the official Salon—was held but once, in 1863, and there was no intention of encouraging avant-garde artists. Ten years before, the emperor himself had openly and violently expressed his irritation at Courbet's *Bathers*. For Count Horace de Vieil-Castel, member of the jury which awarded prizes at the 1853 Salon, Courbet was "the head of the School of the Ignoble." For Count Nieuwerkerke, Director of Fine Arts, who faithfully represented Napoleon III in all respects, realism was "the painting of democrats" which not only displeased but disgusted him. This aversion thus appears to have been more than a matter of taste or cultural backwardness; it was also and above all political. Courbet was the first representative of what other authoritarians were later to call "entartete Kunst," degenerate art—an art, that is, which eluded control and could not be made to serve the ends of a caste, an art which refused to be a tool of the Establishment. Courbet was not the only one to be frowned on by respectable people. Daumier was completely ignored as a painter, and Delacroix had the greatest difficulty in gaining recognition and was never able to win general approbation. It was not so much the manner as the import of their work that offended—the fact that artists, from Delacroix onward, claimed with ever increasing insistence an active share in the making of history.

Delacroix, Daumier and Courbet were the painters who, more than any others, and even before the middle of the century, moved in this direction. The autonomy of their expression, i.e. the autonomy of their artistic language, was the fruit of a conception of creative art that we today would call experimental. They did not aim at an "ideal beauty" conceived in advance as their goal. Beauty was no longer a means of knowledge; rather, the cognitive process worked itself out through the experience which embraced past and present: the past as a tradition of expression to which it is always legitimate to refer; the present as an awareness of action and therefore of history. The latter, obviously, could have nothing to do with Classicism and Neoclassicism, whose day was over; it could have nothing to do with the representation of the Romans of the decadence, as interpreted by Couture, nor even with the young Degas's interpretation of the *Misfortunes of the City of Orleans*, for which Manet reproached him. It was precisely in this respect that the nineteenth century made a definitive break with the ideologies of the past, or better, with the ideology that took its rise with the Counter-Reformation. The work of art no longer had a demonstrative or didactic purpose; it was not intended to frighten, warn or instruct, though it always took effect as a social factor. Its social function, however, was independent of particular institutions; in itself, in the fact of existing and acting as a means of communication, it found its object and its justification. Artistic activity, released from the doctrine of immanence and repudiating a type of representation determined by traditional models, acquired a secular significance which sharply differentiated it not only from religion but from every form of authority. Yet, in bypassing Neoclassicism and referring back, as with Delacroix, to the great Baroque masters, the art of the nineteenth century still retained certain important premises and distinctions; its technique was independent of nature and drew on its own inventive resources.

"In the arts in particular," wrote Delacroix in his *Journal* on March 1, 1859, "deep feeling is required to sustain originality of thought in spite of habits to which talent itself is inevitably inclined to yield." If talent is the endowment which enables an artist to impose a personal style on his vision, it follows that style is not something to be achieved once and for all; it is not a canon but depends on the experience gained through actual work. The problem, then, is to maintain at every working moment a tension which, for the Romantic artist, was emotional. Delacroix, it is clear, was well aware that everything, even history, is resolvable into painting. Later Cézanne was to say that "painting has no other object but itself"; this was no declaration of formalism but a recognition of the autonomy of an activity which, however, is a necessary component of human history.

The relation between Delacroix and Cézanne, and indeed that between Delacroix and the Impressionists, is much closer than would appear from an analysis of their affinities of vision alone. Equally close is the relation between Cézanne and Courbet. The latter too, in his realism, tried to maintain a constant tension, political and therefore emotional also, although of a different tenor from that of Delacroix. For this reason Courbet's social criticism informs not only his pictures on popular themes, but persists even in those on freer subjects, like the portraits and the deliberately provocative nudes in the *Bathers*. His technical procedure could run parallel to, but in any case was different from, that of nature. His realism, at least until about 1855, was accordingly ideological and cannot be described as naturalism. He admitted to having learned much from old and modern masters, but declared himself to be at bottom a "Courbetian." Style, for him too, had to be evolved from experience, and he deliberately set up his painting as an alternative to the codification of the "grand style."

Courbet attacked the society of his time, nettled and provoked it, ridiculing its prejudices and hypocritical moralism. Daumier did so too, but he immersed himself in that society and laid bare its foibles and cruelties. His attacks were more tellingly aimed and went deeper. "Dip into his work," wrote Baudelaire, "and before your eyes will pass, in all its fantastic and arresting reality, all that a great city contains in the way of living monstrosities."

From *Robert Macaire* to *Gens de Justice*, from *Ratapoil* to *Monsieur Prudhomme*, the types of Daumier are those of abjection; not a natural abjection, though one caused by the times and institutions, by the precariousness of moral foundations. In the conflict between Jean Valjean and Javert in *Les Misérables*, Victor Hugo reminds us that nineteenth-century society considered good to be all on one side and evil on the other—the good being in the paternalistic institutions which alone could alleviate evil or eliminate it, always however with a view to consolidating the good. Daumier rebelled against this, and in doing so rebelled against the established order. To its demands he opposed the force of his own judgment, the fruit of his own experience. Once again the artist's work could be defined as an autonomous but necessary activity involving interests and values which are not only aesthetic but moral as well.

"You will never be more than the Daumier of your time"—Couture never realized that in making that taunting remark to his pupil Manet he was uttering a great truth. Like Daumier, Manet saw the needs of the time, saw that they were opposed to technical and ideological stagnation, to the eclectic apathy of academic painters, to the representative generalizations that characterized the prevailing taste. In 1863, speaking of what he called the "naturalist school," Castagnary justified its existence as follows: "It springs from our philosophy which, in reinserting man in the society from which the psychologists had removed him, has taken social life as the main object of our researches. It springs from our ethics which, by substituting the imperative notion of justice for the vague law of love, has settled the relations of men among themselves and thrown new light on the problem of destiny. It springs from our philosophy which, by taking as its principle the equality of individuals, and as its desideratum the equilibration of conditions, has rid the mind of false hierarchies and deceptive distinctions. It springs from all that makes us what we are, all that sets us thinking, moving, acting."

The problem of morality in art, a problem raised above all by the developments of the second half of the nineteenth century, has often been emphasized. It has been discussed by Siegfried Giedion in connection with structural researches in architecture, and by Lionello Venturi in connection with the Impressionists, and Cézanne in particular. It is not a question of an abstract and conventional morality, but one implicit in the demand that the validity of the artistic process should be recognized. The reaction against academicism and eclecticism began from this position. Ruskin and William Morris were its most explicit spokesmen, but the moral imperative is present both in Castagnary and Baudelaire, and it guides the latter's critical approach, his dislike of "the slick and conventional." That the concept is not abstract but springs from an intense social consciousness is shown by the fact that, in most cases, it involves a criticism of institutions. Moreover, Castagnary's reference to psychology, which according to him studied man out of his social context, makes it evident that his outlook is closely connected with that of the Positivists. Auguste Comte excluded psychology from his hierarchy of the sciences. It is important to note that all the writers and critics who showed an interest in realism had come under the influence of the positivist philosophy. They were the heirs of Saint-Simon, and in the new order of society and government which they looked forward to they assigned to art not only a moral but a utilitarian function. They recognized the cardinal importance of the part played by scientists, artists and craftsmen in the life of society, in its progress and enrichment. France, Saint-Simon had written, might lose all the men in her political ranks, and the harm done would be infinitely less than the loss of her scientists, artists and craftsmen.

But the Positivists were not alone in emphasizing the moral implications and the social function of art. In early Victorian England Pugin identified Gothic with the Christian religion and affirmed its superiority over any other style. Pugin was a neo-Gothic architect who never overcame his passion for imitating a style of the past, but his ideas are important for the influence they exerted on Ruskin and Morris. Observing the decadence of art in his time, Ruskin saw the cause of its plight in the social structure. The arch-enemy was the machine, the system of industrial production which had enslaved man, the capitalistic society which had cut the worker off from any personal interest in the product. The result was the aesthetic debasement of that product, and ugliness, declared Ruskin, is an offense against the natural order. The only way to safeguard human

dignity was, according to Morris, to safeguard the dignity of work, to restore to it the attributes of that quality; to do this meant to change the structures of society. Morris was a socialist, of a very different kind from Marx and different from the French democrats and Saint-Simonians; but just as Proudhon had regarded art as inseparable from ethics and philosophy, so Morris refused to consider it apart from ethics, politics and religion. Efforts to raise art again to the greatness of past epochs would be futile without at the same time raising the level of working conditions. The existence of true art in a country, he wrote, depends on much more than the mere presence of two or three artists of genius or talent, or that of a small group of aesthetes or enlightened collectors; an art, he went on to say, can be really great and powerful only if, as in the past, it is the expression of the people's aspiration to beauty.

It is necessary too that that beauty, which logically is not the *ideal* beauty of the classical tradition, should be present in all things, in the products of reinvigorated handicrafts and in the works of a reinvigorated architecture conceived in harmony with those products and above all with the landscape. This was the end to be striven for, and to that end each man must set his hand to the plough. "Neither can we hand our interests in it to a little band of learned men, and bid them seek and discover, and fashion, that we may at last stand by and wonder at the work, and learn a little of how 'twas all done: 'tis we ourselves, each one of us, who must keep watch and ward over the fairness of the earth, and each with his own soul and hand do his due share therein, lest we deliver to our sons a lesser treasure than our fathers left to us" (William Morris).

The idea that aesthetic responsibility is social responsibility informs all Morris's teaching and activities. It was in Victorian England that the first legislation regarding social welfare and town planning was enacted. In 1848 was created the General Board of Health, which exercised control over the water supply, sanitation and gardens; its purpose was to set some order in what Lewis Mumford has called the "paleotechnic inferno." Just after the middle of the century came the first laws on subsidized popular housing, and the first schemes for the orderly planning of towns. But this was a period of unbridled individualism, of blind faith in private enterprise, of a free and arbitrary market economy. Morris called for something quite different—the participation of the people in the creation of their homes and living conditions. He could not be content with the solutions proposed by the Utopians who preceded him, nor even with those which more or less enlightened industrialists were proposing (in 1846 the Richardsons began building a workingmen's village in Ireland). Morris too, convinced as he was that art is of the people and for the people, rejected the principle of authority.

Quality also declined whenever function was subordinated to extraneous elements which prevented the product from achieving its proper purpose. Not only Greenough in America but Labrouste in France proclaimed that form must be determined by function. Viollet-le-Duc himself, in a curious book written for teaching purposes, his *Histoire d'un dessinateur*, recommended a strictly logical sequence to be followed in the designing of any product in order to give it style. "Nature always imparts style to her productions because she proceeds in accordance with a logical order, adopting forms which are the outcome of the purpose in view, and this both in organic and inorganic matter. So if it is intended to create, that is to produce an object belonging to one of the industries of man, it will be well to proceed as nature proceeds, to take into account the purpose of that object and the qualities of the material used to fashion it. Thus a glass or earthenware vessel will not take the form appropriate to a bronze or silver vessel, and iron furniture need not resemble wooden furniture. It is therefore advisable to be thoroughly acquainted with the different industrial processes in order not to depart from them in the design of objects supplied by the different industries."

It is interesting to note that when William Morris was called upon in 1882 to give his opinion before the Royal Commission for Professional Instruction, he expounded similar principles and emphasized how necessary it was for the designer to have gained a thorough knowledge of industrial techniques if he was not to submit designs that were impracticable. It was these men of the second half of the nineteenth century who laid the theoretical and practical bases of modern industrial design. Van de Velde for one has explicitly acknowledged his debt to Morris.

The theory rather than the work of Viollet-le-Duc, as set forth in his *Entretiens sur l'Architecture*, shows the extent to which the foremost French representative of neo-Gothic was alive to the possibilities opened up by new materials, and how through them he discovered the values and the dynamic (as well as static) functions of structures. The great merit of Pierre Francastel in his book *Art et Technique*, which is fundamental for an understanding of this period, is to have shown how, from a study of the structures of the Gothic architecture of the past, Viollet-le-Duc drew a lesson capable of providing technical solutions to the problems of contemporary architecture. He was a rationalist and with him the building process had always to correspond with a process of logical reasoning. The Gothic Revival in England may on the contrary appear to be, and indeed was, ideologically different. Through the return to Gothic the English were striving towards a national style of architectural design, and thus freeing themselves of the age-old Italian influence. However, to English architects too, at least to the best of them (one thinks of what Morris must have learned in the office of George Edmund Street), Gothic appeared as a means of spiritual sublimation through a technical audacity practised with almost mystical fervor. But architecture elsewhere was evolving in an altogether different direction, and already the choice of Romanesque as the basic style—such was Richardson's choice in America—imposed a different conception of space and a more organic simplicity. Even so, the Gothic Revival stimulated interest in an architecture capable of creating open spatial values and contributed in some measure to a new awareness of architectural problems.

The development of architecture was no less beset with difficulties than that of painting, for architects too were trying to work out a more coherent idiom. They realized that out of new materials new structures could and must be created, transcending the old eclecticisms, whether classicizing, neo-Gothic or neo-Baroque in tendency. Moreover the ideological affinities between forward-looking artists in both fields are evident. Viollet-le-Duc's reference to the organic and inorganic patterns of nature found echoes in positivist culture. Labrouste's designs for the Bibliothèque Nationale in Paris are the concrete outcome of an experiment conducted with new materials, a testing out not only of their static and dynamic but of their expressive possibilities. With his "real allegories" Courbet was seeking to establish the principle of the organic reality of form and representation, a reality determined by the creative act. And, after Courbet, the Impressionists were not romantic dreamers intent on recording a fleeting, subjective impression; their approach was a calculated means of giving a precise and by no means ephemeral structure to perceptions, to a localization of the phenomena with which the artist established a dialectical and no longer acquiescent relationship. Impressionist painting has nothing metaphysical about it, nor do the researches of nineteenth-century engineers. Rejecting the widespread notion that art, whatever the form it may take, must develop along the lines laid down by a style borrowed from the past, and thereby rebelling against an authoritarian and unhistorical injunction, both artists and architects saw the necessity—seen already moreover by Delacroix—of creating an idiom no longer conditioned by national differences, but one with a common appeal to all men without distinction. Thus were laid the foundations on which all subsequent forms of artistic expression have arisen, and which are still today an indispensable part of our cultural heritage.

WITH STEAM AND THE BIBLE

Industrial and commercial power, together with the political authority which voiced that power and represented it on the plane of institutions, created a "liturgy" of its own with the great trade fairs and expositions. Planned at first on a national scale, they became international or world fairs beginning in 1851, and remain so today. Here the technical advances, commercial enterprise and colonial resources of each country were exhibited and compared; to do that, and do it in an increasingly spectacular style, cost a lot of money, but it was a matter of prestige. World fairs were inaugurated and visited by kings, queens and presidents; they displayed to a dazzled public the wealth of the ruling class, its taste in art, and the effects on city and country of "good government": they were a typical product of the capitalist economy. True, they provided an unquestionable stimulus to architectural design— but not always, and the World's Columbian Exposition held at Chicago in 1893 is the most signal failure in this respect. In general, however, the buildings designed to house the exhibits gave a pretty clear indication of the progress made by architects in working out a new style in harmony with the new materials which technology placed at their disposal.

The great fairs also benefited the so-called minor or applied arts, for they raised the problem of a more functional and less decorative design for objects and revealed, sometimes dramatically, the harm caused by the cleavage between taste and technique which had occurred when mass production dealt the death blow to the handicrafts. The fairs brought home the fact that industrial products cannot be cast in a borrowed style, that a steam engine in Gothic shape is an absurdity, that objects and machines produced by industry must be given a design stylistically and functionally adapted to the purpose they are intended to serve. But it was a long uphill struggle before this goal was reached; in the way stood a laissez-faire economy demanding a steady increase in production and an uninformed public blind as yet to its true interests—a public prompt to express its admiration for the palatial buildings housing the displays of industry and machinery but indifferent to the subsequent demolition of those buildings.

If Ruskin and Morris were so earnest in their denunciations of the factory system and their rejection of a civilization based on machinery, it was because of the horror they felt at the spread of the industrial blight and its deadening effect on the aesthetic sensibilities of the mass of consumers. The bad taste increasingly rife and, according to Morris, invading every home, and the "loss of any instinct for beauty," were caused by a commercialism whose sole ambition was to turn out a cheap product for the widest possible market. As a practising artist and craftsman Morris discovered that the colors supplied by industry were apt to change hue unpredictably shortly after they were used. But his courageous activity, which led him to revive the traditional techniques of craftsmanship, to master them with his own hands and even to concoct himself the dyes he needed for printed textiles, was hampered by the inexorable laws of a capitalist economy. The revival of the old handicrafts required time and money, and Morris found it impossible to supply the articles he designed and made at competitive prices.

This in no way diminishes the validity of his efforts, and the lesson of Morris and the Arts and Crafts movement proved a positive and fruitful one, even before the turn of the century, for those who took up where he left off and who, convinced of the need for well-designed objects and industrial products, imposed a style on them.

For Morris was no Utopian. To a social and industrial order which considered progress only from a technological point of view and subordinated or sacrificed all else to that end, causing "the reckless destruction of the natural beauty of the earth," he opposed a comprehensive vision of the world and society and saw clearly, through all their complexity, the many improvements they were open to in the interrelated domains of art, morals and institutions. In short, to the ideological sterility of industrial production, he opposed an ideology fully conscious of all its constructive possibilities. Between those two worlds, thus contrasted (at least in appearance), some agreement should be possible, but not on the assumption that the artist, whether practising a major or a minor art (a distinction, by the way, that Morris refused to recognize), should surrender his dignity or his ability to rise above an egalitarian uniformity. The problem raised by Morris was a *universal* one; that it concerned not only the British economy to which it directly referred, but that of all countries, was clearly shown by the products sent in to the world fairs and exhibitions which followed each other closely throughout the second half of the nineteenth century.

An exhibition of limited scope had been held in Prague in 1791, but the idea of a competitive display of goods showing a country's productive capacity was born in France under the Directory. François de Neufchâteau, Minister of the Interior, organized an exhibition of the industrial products and handicrafts of France. It was therefore purely national in character; in fact its avowed aim was "to deal a deadly blow at English industry." It opened on September 19, 1798, in the Champ-de-Mars, being held in a rectangular area bounded by fifty-eight arcades, the work of the architect François Chalgrin, who later designed the Arc de Triomphe. It is noteworthy that, from the start, the fair grounds and exhibition halls were entrusted to an architect. Probably the very idea of such a display derived from the Salons of painting and sculpture which had long been held in France. Further exhibitions took place in Paris (but not annually as was originally intended): in 1801 and 1802 in the gardens of the Louvre and in 1806 on the esplanade in front of the Invalides. (In 1801 painters and sculptors were also invited to exhibit their works but they refused.) More were held in Paris some years later, though always of a strictly national character: in 1818, 1819, 1823, 1827, 1834 (this time in the Place de la Concorde), 1839, 1844 and 1849 (these last in the Champs-Elysées). By this time the limiting restrictions on exhibitors were being removed. As early as 1830 a customs official, Boucher de Perthes,

had expressed the hope that the exhibitions would become international, but the idea was opposed by manufacturers and even in 1849 the French minister of commerce was compelled to abandon plans for an international exhibition.

Local trade fairs had also been held in England, and in London in 1851 the first "great exhibition of the works of industry of all nations" took place, the moving spirits being Prince Albert and an enlightened civil servant, Sir Henry Cole. The building erected for the exhibition was one of original design, rising above eclecticism in its coherent structural use of metal and glass: this was the Crystal Palace designed by Sir Joseph Paxton. It was in London too, thanks again to Sir Henry Cole, that some approach was made to the problems raised by the relation between industrial production and the applied arts. The same problems were dealt with in the report drawn up by the Comte de Laborde, French delegate to the exhibition, and published in Paris in 1856.

The Crystal Palace, erected in Hyde Park, housed the first world's fair to feature the products of modern industry; its success, even financially, was spectacular, beyond that of any subsequent fair. The exhibits fell into thirty different categories embracing all forms of production: means of locomotion, agricultural and industrial machinery, architectural designs, statues, furniture, optical and musical instruments, carpets, textiles and so on. The public seemed as pleased with the results as the producers and manufacturers , and this is just what was wanted at a time when a "consumer civilization" was taking its first decisive steps. More and more, technical progress was identified with human progress. Advancing technology brought benefits that all could see and touch, and few stopped to consider what the price of those benefits might be. "With steam and the Bible," we read in Tallis's account of the Great Exhibition, "the English traverse the globe." Prince Albert, busy with plans for a house for a working class family also to be erected in Hyde Park, expressed the comforting conviction that "we are living in a period of most wonderful transition, which tends rapidly to the accomplishment of that great end to which indeed all history points, the realization of the unity of mankind." And under the inspiration of Cole the prince consort emphasized the need to reconcile the fine arts with the products of industry.

But in this respect the Great Exhibition was a failure. The works of art that figured in it—and they were confined to sculpture—were the dreariest examples imaginable of the taste of that day, giving no hint of the developments to come; Tallis aptly described them as "an agglomeration of artistic delinquencies." Above all the exhibition showed up the now irreparable breach between art and industry. Only Pugin's Medieval Court, containing objects designed by Pugin himself, metalwork by John Hardman, ceramics by Herbert Minton, furniture by John Grace, and wood carvings by George Myers, presented an appearance of unity; but the principle of design followed throughout was that of the neo-Gothic dear to Pugin. For the rest, the products displayed by the different nations were marked by an unmitigated eclecticism, an incredible mixture of styles ancient and modern, overloaded with decorative elements. The decline of the handicrafts was all too evident: vases and ceramics, porcelain wares, carpets, textiles and furniture were all in the worst possible taste. The manufacturers had no remedy to offer, for they were concerned with quantity, not quality. Locomotives, telescopes and machinery in general did have forms well adapted to their purpose, but the clocks, the dishes produced by new technical methods, even the looms that turned out over-ornate fabrics, were covered with an abundance of superfluous decorations; iron bedsteads and skates were embellished with swans' heads; knives, forks and spoons had handles in the form of languidly posed figures. All this was in contrast with the structural fitness of the Crystal Palace itself. Clearly industry had not the faintest conception of what unity of design meant. Prevailing tastes were pandered to at their worst and the miseducation of the public went steadily ahead.

Yet out of this situation sprang the forces of renewal. Ruskin loathed the Crystal Palace and all it contained. But Cole and other personalities of his group thought differently. Recent students of this period—Nikolaus Pevsner, Siegfried Giedion, Pierre Francastel—have rightly drawn attention to the merits, and the limitations, of the theories and practice of Cole, Owen Jones, Richard Redgrave and Matthew Digby Wyatt. In 1855 Cole founded the South Kensington (now Victoria and Albert) Museum as a showplace for the applied arts of all countries, of both East and West. In 1856 Owen Jones, who had been responsible for the interior decoration of the Crystal Palace, published his *Grammar of Ornament*. Neither shrank from the dawning world of science and industry, they sought on the contrary to reconcile it with the arts. Though attracted by Pugin's ideas, they realized that in applying the new techniques it was useless seeking inspiration in the styles of the past. Like Pugin, they felt that ornament must not be something abstract and superadded, that it must rather be simplified as much as possible. Richard Redgrave, in his *Manual of Design* (1876), laid it down that the function of applied arts must be utilitarian. Directly connected with these ideas was the work of Gottfried Semper (who was employed for a time in London by Prince Albert) and his theory of essential forms—forms that can only be determined by the techniques and materials used. In proof of the fact that nineteenth-century thought laid the basis of the most modern methods of critical inquiry, we need only add that Semper's ideas exerted some influence, admittedly limited, on one of the founders of the criticism of pure perception, Alois Riegl.

Following the example of London, New York organized an international exhibition in 1853; it too was housed in a Crystal Palace, but one that lacked the structural harmony of Paxton's building, and on which a dome was superimposed. Paris in turn sponsored in 1855 a "universal exposition of the products of agriculture, industry and the fine arts." A Palais de l'Industrie was erected in the Champs-Elysées, with an adjoining Galerie des Machines, and a Palais des Beaux-Arts in the Carré Marigny. In the four years that had passed since the first international exhibition in London, startling technical advances had been made: not only new machines and new uses for them, but new systems of production and great forward strides in metallurgy, in chemistry, in the development of photography. At the Paris World's Fair, as at the Great Exhibition, the exhibits were divided into thirty categories. But as far as applied arts and handicrafts were concerned, though there was a greater refinement in some of the objects exhibited, especially French furniture, no very notable changes had occurred since 1851. For the first time, however, the rules governing the exhibition, announced on June 22, 1853, provided for a special section devoted to art, in the conviction that "improvements in industry are closely bound up with those in the fine arts"; even lithographs and chromolithographs were accordingly exhibited. Still, this wider scope was more apparent than real, for the works shown in the Palais des Beaux-Arts had been carefully screened by Count Nieuwerkerke and a committee which, while also including Ingres and Delacroix, was largely composed of members of the Institute. Courbet's *Funeral at Ornans* and *The Painter's Studio* were both rejected, though eleven other pictures of his were accepted. Determining to hold his own show, he rented a vacant lot and had the architect Félix Isabey erect a pavilion for him in which he exhibited some forty paintings and a few drawings; and he had a catalogue printed which he prefaced with a declaration of his creed of "realism."

Baudelaire on that occasion described the artist as "a powerful workman," and this is enough to show the poet's profound understanding of the true nature of art in his time. The 1855 World's Fair is memorable not only for the secession of Courbet, whose example was followed on a later occasion by Manet, but also for its exhibition of paintings by Ingres and Delacroix and Baudelaire's review of that exhibition, one of his finest writings on art. As for the rest, who remembers or has even heard of Muller's *Appeal of Those Condemned to Death under the Terror* or Cabanel's *Christian Martyr*? Couture's *Romans of the Decadence* is now in the Louvre; it may stand as a dread example of a kind of art already stale and anachronistic by the middle of the nineteenth century. Yet such was the style of art preferred by public and ruling class alike.

No valid comparison is possible between the ideas of Morris and Baudelaire; the cultural traditions which shaped them were too different, and so were the guiding interests and backgrounds of the two men. Morris could draw on the legacy of eighteenth-century English thought, and his emphasis on enthusiasm as an essential ingredient of good work derives not only from Ruskin but directly from Shaftesbury. Baudelaire had that luminous clarity which is typical of French thought at its best; while he shunned mysticism of any kind, he felt that the basis of just criticism must be emotional but that the thinking mind must subsequently intervene. He had moreover a wonderfully keen insight into works of art, grasping at once their merits or shortcomings, their possible openings on to the future. Though a poet first and foremost, he never asked of painting the equivalent of a literary sensation. There are of course analogies between the two men. For Baudelaire too the artistic process, arising as it does out of personal experience, was very different from a mechanical process. In his comments on the 1855 World's Fair he reminded his readers that "painting is an evocation, a magical operation" and put them on their guard against "the modern idea of progress applied to the fine arts"; this he considered a "grotesque idea," an "infatuation symptomatic of a decadence already all too visible." It was time to explode these notions and re-establish the logical order of things, "to read history aright" and open the eyes of "zoocratic and industrial philosophers" to the "differences which characterize the phenomena of the physical and the moral world, of the natural and the supernatural." He saw in art a profound moral imperative which made it necessary to any society worthy of the name. Baudelaire visited the fair but spoke only of the works of art; he took no interest in the machinery or even in the handicrafts; his testimony, even though indirect, nevertheless throws a flood of light on the crucial problem of the moment. In the relations between art and technics, or better between artistic ideology and technology, the role of art must not be a subordinate one. The artist claimed his rightful place, on an equal footing, and not out of pride but because he was convinced that the avenues of knowledge opened up by his work were as indispensable to the development of man as those of science.

The truth of this was in fact dimly realized by the organizers of the Paris World's Fair, though there was little they could do, had they wanted to, against the reactionary machinations of the Institute. The program laid down in June 1853 acknowledged that in France "industry owed a great deal to the fine arts," and the committee for architecture included such men as Viollet-le-Duc and Labrouste. In this respect the 1855 World's Fair marked an advance on the Great Exhibition of 1851, for it was concerned to establish a basis of comparison between the two fields of endeavor; no such basis had been offered in London. Although on the whole rejecting the work of those avant-garde artists who are today their pride and glory, the French always saw to it that art figured alongside industry in all subsequent exhibitions of this kind, some of which, like that of 1889, were architecturally among the most important of the century.

The next great world's fair was held in London in 1862, but it was not so successful as that of 1851. In 1873 there was an International Exhibition in Vienna, in the woodlands of the Prater; the main building was a great rotunda designed by the English architect Scott Russell, but it was marred by a profusion of decorations and stuccoes. The Paris exhibition of 1867 was an event of world-wide importance, and it was followed by others, after the fall of the Empire, in 1878, 1889 and 1900. The last decade of the century saw a spate of international exhibitions all over Europe, in Antwerp, Budapest, Kiel, Lyons, Geneva, Stuttgart, Berlin, then Brussels, Leipzig, Stockholm and still other cities. In the United States a Centennial Exhibition was held in Philadelphia in 1876 to celebrate the one hundredth anniversary of American independence. There were five great pavilions: the Main Building, the Hall of Machinery, the Memorial Hall devoted to the fine arts, the Flower Palace, and the Agricultural Building. The four hundredth anniversary of the discovery of America was commemorated in Chicago in 1893 by a World's Columbian Exposition; it too was divided into different pavilions which, with the exception of Sullivan's Transportation Building, marked a sharp regression in architectural design, and in taste (gondolas and gondoliers were imported from Venice). A great exhibition was also held at Atlanta in 1895—the Cotton States and International Exposition.

Of all these displays, those organized in Paris were undoubtedly the most significant. In 1867 Eiffel was already at work alongside the engineer Krantz. The main building, intended at first to be circular in imitation of the terrestial globe, was a large oval comprising halls devoted to the fine arts, the history of human labor, dress, furniture, food, and what was styled "arts usuels ou machines." On display were the plans for the Suez Canal and an infinity of products described as "both serviceable and cheap." One of the first prizes, however, was awarded to the Sèvres porcelain manufactory for wares whose decorations tediously kept to the styles of the past. Held in the Champ-de-Mars, the 1867 World's Fair was divided into ten sections grouping ninety-five categories of products. Courbet, as he had done in 1855, sent in three pictures to the official exhibition, to which was added a fourth owned by the Imperial family, but he showed a hundred and fifty others in a pavilion built at his own expense. Manet followed suit and showed some fifty paintings of his own in a private pavilion. The Paris World's Fair of 1878 was held in the palace of the Trocadéro, erected for the occasion, and in a metal building put up in the Champ-de-Mars. The hall of machinery designed by the engineer De Dion was the finest and boldest thing of all. The jury which selected works of art not only rejected Manet, Millet, Rousseau, Troyon, Decamps, Barye and Ricard, but dismissed the very idea of a Delacroix retrospective.

To commemorate the centenary of the French Revolution, another World's Fair was held in Paris in 1889 with peace and progress as its keynote. Among the novelties were the Eiffel Tower and that masterpiece of nineteenth-century architecture, the Galerie des Machines of Dutert and Contamin. Antonin Proust, Roger Marx and Georges Petit, two critics and a dealer, all three discerning and open-minded, organized the exhibition of works of art with the obvious purpose of redressing, in so far as possible, the wrongs committed in the past. It included this time a representative selection of the best French artists of the century: David, Prud'hon, Delacroix, Ingres, Millet, Corot, Rousseau, Daumier, Courbet, Daubigny, up to Puvis de Chavannes and Bastien-Lepage. But Roger Marx also succeeded in including fourteen pictures by Manet (among them *The Fifer*, *Le Bon Bock* and *In a Boat*), four by Fantin-Latour, three by Monet and two by Pissarro. The collector Victor Choquet was asked to lend some period furniture, and did so on condition that a canvas of his by Cézanne, the *Hanged Man's House*, should also figure in the exhibition. It was intended to set aside a whole room for Degas, but he, like Renoir, declined to take part. In the foreign section, among a surfeit of academic works, there were a few pictures by the Italian Macchiaioli, five by Fattori, two by Signorini and two of those executed in France by Serafino De Tivoli; two paintings by Giovanni Segantini were also shown. Gauguin, who had not been invited, followed the earlier example of Courbet and Manet and held a private showing at the Café Volpini, hard by the fair grounds, together with Anquetin, Emile Bernard, Laval, Daniel de Monfreid, Fauché and Roy.

As for objects of interior decoration, a distinct improvement could be noted: the Sèvres manufactory had simplified the forms of its wares; Gallé exhibited vases of faceted crystal and cups decorated with figures and flowers, Tiffany enameled gold flowers and even a crystal vase mounted with stones and gold filigree, whose elegance of line pointed the way to a new style already typical of Art Nouveau. In the Champ-de-Mars Charles Garnier, the architect of the neo-Baroque Paris Opera, erected the buildings where the "History of the Human Home" was illustrated in three sections: prehistoric dwellings, dwellings of historical times and "contemporary dwellings of primitive civilizations, of peoples who have lived outside the general movement of mankind, on which they have exerted no influence." Progress was still equated with technological development and a journalist covering the exhibition wrote: "Certain it is that at the end of this scientific century the masterpiece of progress must be sought for in the Galerie des Machines. And there we find it. To the left of the main hall that leads to this vast department, we see above all the machines in motion a name plate on which is written 'Edison.' People crowd around them. At least a hundred phonographs are in motion..." Mechanical and scientific gadgets were already appearing in the form of toys. On exhibit too were dirigibles driven by steam engines or electric motors, designed by Tissandier, Vicini, Giffard, Dupuy-de-Lôme and Krebs. One of the star attractions was the terrestrial globe of Villard and Cotard. Men saw new horizons before them, but already critical minds were at work demolishing the optimistic faith in progress which had largely characterized later nineteenth-century thought. In 1874 Emile Boutroux published his essay *De la contingence des lois de la nature* and in 1889 Bergson published his *Essai sur les données immédiates de la conscience*. By now the identification of science and technology was beginning to seem less and less legitimate.

Three years later the French legislature approved plans for another exhibition which, in the words of the minister of commerce Jules Roche, was to "constitute the synthesis and determine the philosophy of the nineteenth century." The 1900 World's Fair was larger than any previously held, its buildings extending from the Place de la Concorde to the Champs-Elysées (with the Grand-Palais of Deglane and Louvet and the Petit-Palais of Girault), the Trocadéro and the Champ-de-Mars. Paris was refurbished to welcome the new century: a new bridge, the Pont Alexandre III, was thrown across

the Seine in a single metal arch; the Métro was coming into operation; and the new Gare d'Orléans was opened. In charge of the exhibition was Alfred Picard, a thoroughbred technician who declared: "In the forefront stand education and training: these are the portals through which man enters life, these are the head and fount of all progress." Great prominence was given to masterpieces of painting, engraving and sculpture. There was a retrospective showing of earlier French art, with particular emphasis on industrial and religious art. There was a centennial and decennial exhibition, organized by Roger Marx; in both figured works by the Impressionists, including Bazille.

The 1900 World's Fair fulfilled its declared purpose of presenting a synthesis of the activities and progress of the previous century. At the same time it opened a window on the future and demonstrated that a great many issues canvassed in the recent past had been or were about to be resolved. Admittedly none of the buildings reached the level of the Galerie des Machines of 1889; most were spoiled by the exoticism and eclecticism of the decorations. Among the projects set afoot there was even one by L. Tropey-Bailly which proposed to modify the Eiffel Tower by adding four Gothic towers to the base; luckily it was not accepted. The Grand-Palais and Petit-Palais were striking illustrations of the architectural compromise that had been arrived at, and the entrance to the exhibition, erected in the Place de la Concorde by Binet, was flanked by two minarets. There were some spectacular buildings like the Château d'Eau and the Palais de l'Electricité, but the value of the Eiffel Tower as a visual landmark was enhanced by the prospect opened up by the new thoroughfare across the Pont Alexandre III. The range of exhibits and attractions was extraordinarily wide: art exhibitions, sideshows, a reconstruction of the Vieux Paris, and a Rue des Nations where, in the British pavilion, a tapestry by William Morris was on display. In the way of furniture, those of Bigaux and the dining room designed by Plumet and Selmersheim were of outstanding quality. Art Nouveau not only stamped an aesthetic individuality on many objects, but at its best, following the lessons of Morris, went far to solve the problem of imposing a new distinction of style on industrial production. By now automobile design had gone beyond the imitation of horse-drawn carriages; already cars had distinctive forms of their own, indeed a beauty of their own, appropriate to their function. Most important of all, the idea of progress had ceased to be an inhuman abstraction; it had come to be considered strictly in relation to human endeavor with none of the "rigorous detachment" later spoken of by Husserl. The nineteenth century thus came to a close in a new moral climate, transmitting its "potentialities" for the better use of the twentieth, on which it strongly impressed the necessity and validity of its experience and actions.

Signs of that new moral climate were everywhere evident at the Turin Exhibition of 1902, which was entirely devoted to modern decoration and thus did not include the products of industry. It offered a survey and summing up of the results achieved in the arts of design both in Europe and the United States in the closing years of the nineteenth century. This was perhaps the high-water mark of Art Nouveau,

and the Exhibition brought before a larger public than ever before, and one certainly more open-minded, a display of decorative art and architecture deliberately designed in terms of a particular and highly characteristic style. The pavilions were the work of the Italian architects D'Aronco and Rigotti; the artists and craftsmen represented included Morris, Horta, Hoffmann, Behrens, Walter Crane, Ashbee, Voysey, Gallé, Tiffany, and the Glasgow group headed by Mackintosh. For all its inevitable limitations, its decorative excesses, and the literary and decadent commonplaces of the less original artists, the Turin Exhibition offered a welcome opportunity for comparison and confrontation between the various national "schools" grouped together under the aegis of Art Nouveau; above all it showed clearly that for the first time in a century an art style had taken root over a wide area and, regardless of frontiers, had firmly established itself as an international style.

1

THE GREAT EXHIBITIONS

None of the buildings erected for the great international exhibitions deserves to rank among the finest achievements of nineteenth-century architecture. They are however, even though they have been destroyed, valuable landmarks and points of reference in tracing the development of a new style of architecture based on new methods of construction. Sir Joseph Paxton's Crystal Palace built in London to house the Great Exhibition of 1851, together with Dutert and Contamin's Galerie des Machines and the Eiffel Tower, both erected for the Paris World's Fair of 1889, represent three such landmarks. Breaking away from the eclecticism and ponderous monumentality typical of current taste, forced indeed by the nature of such constructions to design them on the simplest lines and make the best possible use of materials, these architects and engineers aimed at functional buildings adapted to their intended purpose. The public accepted them as it accepted industrial products; with a great show of enthusiasm, but without any critical participation and in most cases without realizing that these works were bringing about a revolution in architectural design.

For the building destined to house the Great Exhibition of 1851, an open competition was organized and 247 designs were submitted. First prize was awarded to Hector Horeau, but his project was not executed as the Commission insisted on the use

PARIS WORLD'S FAIR OF 1878: MAIN ENTRANCE.
CONTEMPORARY PHOTOGRAPH BY CHEVOJON.

PARIS WORLD'S FAIR OF 1889: THE GALERIE DES MACHINES OF DUTERT AND CONTAMIN.
CONTEMPORARY PHOTOGRAPH BY CHEVOJON.

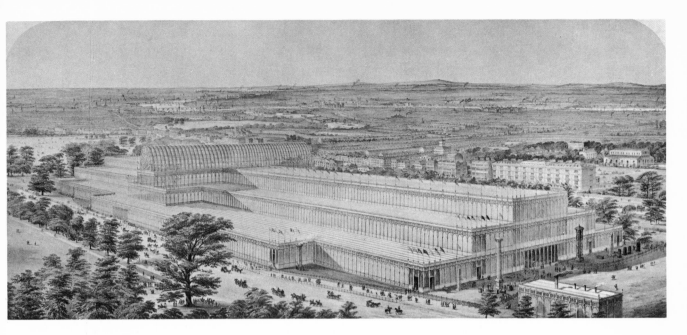

THE GREAT EXHIBITION OF 1851 IN LONDON: SIR JOSEPH PAXTON'S CRYSTAL PALACE.
CONTEMPORARY LITHOGRAPH. (VICTORIA AND ALBERT MUSEUM PHOTO, CROWN COPYRIGHT)

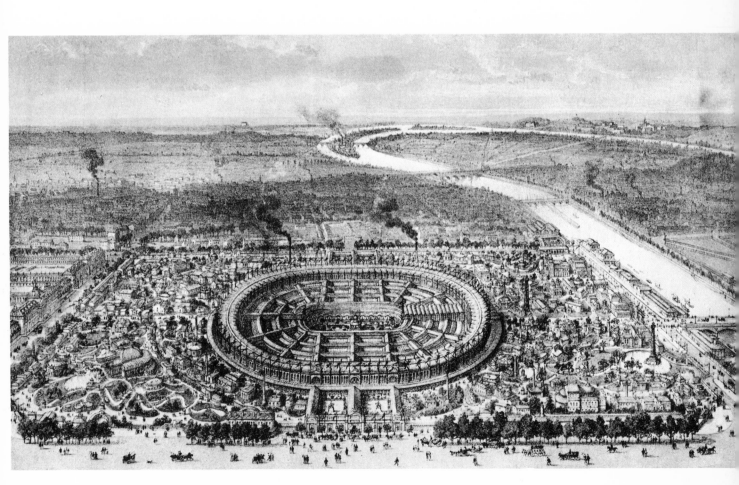

PARIS WORLD'S FAIR OF 1867: GENERAL VIEW.
PRINT FROM "PARIS-GUIDE PAR LES PRINCIPAUX ÉCRIVAINS DE FRANCE," PARIS 1867.

of materials which could be re-employed afterwards; Paxton's project, submitted after the competition had closed, met this condition. His designs for the Crystal Palace (as the building was christened by *Punch*) were completed on June 11, 1850; the first columns, of cast iron, were put in place on September 26 and by January 1851 the building was finished and ready. Measuring 1851 feet in length (the numerical coincidence was deliberate) and covering a ground area of some 800,000 square feet, it had been put up within six months—an amazing feat at that time. But Paxton had modeled it on the greenhouse and it consisted of a simple system of small standardized units, designed with a view to being easily dismantled and re-employed afterwards; Paxton gave no thought to ornament, leaving it to Owen Jones to decorate the interior as he saw fit.

The structural members were manufactured in Birmingham and fitted together on the site in London. Everything was simplified in the extreme. The supporting columns were hollow, thus serving to drain off rain-water from the glass roofing, which had been assembled in a very simple way devised by Paxton: a small trolley running along the girders carried the workmen who installed the panes of plate glass. The building was designed on a longitudinal plan; the transept in the center, not provided for in the original plan, was only added in order to bring several trees within the building. There were three main entrances, seventy exits and ten double stairways. As regards the interior decoration, the vertical members were painted in blue, curving members in yellow, and the lower part of the structural framework in red. When the exhibition was over the Crystal Palace, built in Hyde Park, was dismantled and moved to Sydenham where it stood until 1937, when it was destroyed by fire.

Paxton's Crystal Palace was the prototype of many subsequent fair buildings. The Palais de l'Industrie however, erected for the Paris World's Fair of 1855, represents a compromise: the internal metal framework, erected by the engineer Barrault, was completely encased in heavy stone walls designed by the architect Viel. At the Paris World's Fair of 1867 the main hall formed a gigantic ellipse including a Galerie des Machines—twice as high as the other six galleries—designed by the engineer J. B. Krantz, ably assisted by the young Eiffel. At the 1878 World's Fair, in addition to the Palais du Trocadéro designed by the architects Bourdais and Davioud and built of stone, Krantz erected a Palais de l'Industrie

PARIS WORLD'S FAIR OF 1889: GENERAL VIEW. PRINT

THE WORLD'S COLUMBIAN EXPOSITION AT CHICAGO IN 1893.
ORIGINAL PHOTOGRAPH. (CHICAGO ARCHITECTURAL PHOTO CO.)

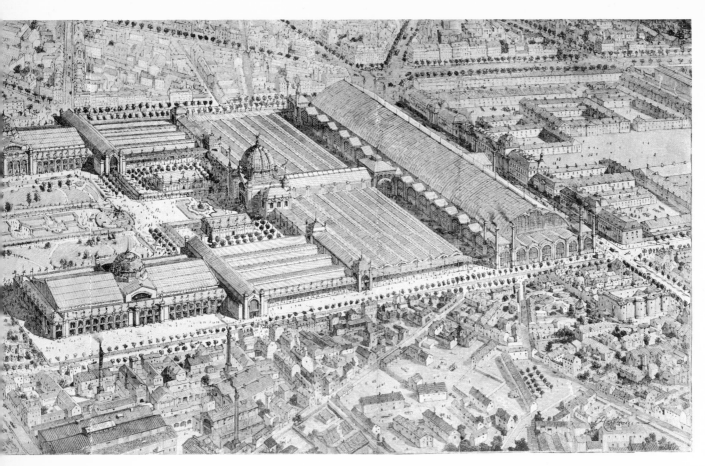

PARIS WORLD'S FAIR OF 1900: THE ESPLANADE DES INVALIDES.
CONTEMPORARY PHOTOGRAPH BY CHEVOJON.

designed by L. Hardy; the two vestibules were constructed by Eiffel. The Galerie des Machines of the engineer De Dion exploited all the possibilities of metal structures, with a network of straight and curving girders which absorbed the stresses without the assistance of either tie bars or outer buttresses.

The Paris World's Fair of 1889 was notable for the Eiffel Tower and for the Galerie des Machines of Dutert and Contamin. The latter, with a span of 377 feet and a length of 1378 feet, forming an immense hall without any central supporting members, was a brilliant application of the new building methods; contemporaries were disconcerted by its entirely new conception of space. Even more disconcerting at first was the Eiffel Tower, which has now come to be an irreplaceable feature of the Parisian skyline. As Ruskin had protested against the Crystal Palace, so now Zola, Gounod, Meissonier, Maupassant and Bonnat, among many other artists and intellectuals, protested against the Eiffel Tower. Even the Goncourt brothers pronounced it an abomination; for them an iron monument could not be a human monument.

True, Eiffel conceived his Tower as a monument, but, it must be added, as a monument of pure structure. The result was in a sense ambiguous because of the decorative embellishments (which however were eliminated) and certain concessions made to prevailing tastes; yet it remains a major achievement, revealing a new conception of space in terms of metal structures which give, as it were, dynamic and chromatic accents to the space. It is important too for the technical innovations of its construction, for, as Eiffel said himself, it soars into the heavens as a counter-force opposed to the force of the winds. It is, furthermore, a remarkable example of collaboration between Eiffel, its designer, the architect Sauvestre and the engineers Nougier and Koechlin.

The Paris Fair of 1889 was the last of the century whose buildings can be said to have achieved a perfect architectural coherence. The 1900 Fair reverted to a decorative and eclectic compromise. Things were even worse outside France. The World's Columbian Exposition at Chicago in 1893, with its reversion to a staid classicist style of architecture, represented a betrayal of the ideals embodied in the work of the great Chicago architects. This was realized at the time by Louis Sullivan, who foresaw that "the damage wrought to this country by the Chicago World's Fair will last half a century."

ARTISTS WITHOUT LAURELS AND APES OF SENTIMENT

During the nineteenth century there was a divorce between art and the public which even today, far from being remedied, is still a fateful legacy. In an attempt to establish the precise moment when this break took place, Siegfried Giedion has suggested that its origin lies in the "Proclamation of the Freedom of Labor" issued during the French Revolution on March 17, 1791. From then on, though ostensibly free, the artist gradually lost "his natural contact with society. Industrialization coincided with this loss of contact" (Giedion). As a result, the majority of artists yielded to the temptation to give the public anything that might flatter it, pictures that raised no particular problems and, by invoking the authority of some great master of the past, could not offend against accepted tastes and standards.

Thus was born, during the first half of the nineteenth century, "the art of the Salons, of the gold medals and the Prix de Rome, official art... the art of critics who pandered to the public, critics who saw nothing and had no desire to see anything." This happened because the great democratic principles of the Revolution were not really put into practice, or not for long. Though the Proclamation of the Freedom of Labor did emancipate the artist in some ways, doing away with compulsory residence in "privileged places" and breaking the stranglehold of the organized guilds, yet it offered no alternative, merely replacing the guilds by an academic body whose members were elected by other academicians under the control and censorship of the state.

Furthermore the Proclamation of the Freedom of Labor coincided with the peak of Neoclassicism, an aesthetic that had undermined the traditional attitude of sympathy and open-mindedness towards contemporary works of art: artists were now expected to imitate the models of classical art, which were held up as an unsurpassable ideal. For the Neoclassicist the problem of the artist's relations to the public did not exist. David was the official painter first of the Revolution, then of the Empire. He did not have to conform to the prevailing taste; on the contrary, he formed that taste himself and not only in painting. The break came with the passing of Neoclassicism. Then a gulf opened up between artist and public that was never to be bridged; it widened steadily during the Restoration. "My opinions in painting," wrote Stendhal in 1824, "are those of the extreme left wing." The fact that he uses political terminology in attacking the "school of David" shows how far things had gone by this time. On one side was a conservative ruling class with its clique of hangers-on (what today we would call the Establishment), on the other an art world that claimed its autonomy but for that very reason was regarded with suspicion and relegated to the fringe of society.

By the middle of the century conditions had not improved. Indeed they had grown worse, and the relations between artist and public had been further embittered by industrialization, now in full swing. Though the public seemed happy enough to accept machine-made products in daily life and was enthusiastic over new inventions and discoveries, it made a sharp distinction between technology and the arts. An engineer was a technician, not an artist, and architecture was the province of draftsmen. Just as paintings continued to be divided into a hierarchy according to subject matter, history painting being considered a nobler form of art than landscape, so in architecture "artistic quality" was recognized only in ornate, palatial buildings in a Neoclassic, Neo-Gothic or Neo-Baroque style, perforce of stone or marble, with columns and entablatures, pinnacles and pilasters. Stone was felt to be a noble material which gave a sense of permanence, while metal was thought of as a makeshift; stone meant dignity, metal the merely functional or perhaps even the pinch of necessity. Aesthetic standards being what they were at that time, there could be no compromise between the two materials. A conservatory could have a metal framework, or Les Halles in Paris, the

Crystal Palace in London, a factory, a library and of course a bridge. But a government building had to be in stone. If a "work of art" needed a metal structure, it was masked and hidden from view. Canina, an Italian architect, even designed some "embellishments" to improve on Paxton's Crystal Palace. But probably the most notorious example of this notion is the Statue of Liberty in New York harbor. The French sculptor Bartholdi could never have erected a statue over a hundred and fifty feet high without the internal metal armature designed for it by Eiffel. But there is no relation between the internal structure and the outward form; the sculptor took no account of the possibilities offered him by the engineer. The modeling of the statue is like a heavy shift veiling the nudity of its actual structure, and no one entering New York harbor today has the least suspicion that Eiffel's genius stands imprisoned by Bartholdi's chaste figure within the empty shell of a statue unvitalized by any contact with history.

In March 1838 Alexandre Decamps wrote in *Le National*: "Works of art of too independent an originality, of too bold an execution, offend the eyes of our bourgeois society, whose narrow outlook cannot comprehend the mighty conceptions of genius nor the generous impulses of a love for one's fellow men. Public opinion goes its way benightedly, blind to all that is great and all that stands above it." So compromise was inevitable. Romantic painting —apart of course from its commanding personalities—petered out because it lapsed into a vein of literary sentimentalism calculated to appeal to the majority. The Goncourts noted that, by about 1840, Romanticism had "ended up in a kind of exhaustion and impotence." Baudelaire showed his awareness of this decline when, in discussing Ary Scheffer and the "apes of sentiment" *(les singes du sentiment)*, he pointed out how the painter had "aped" everybody, Delacroix and the colorists, the French draftsmen and the neo-Christian school of Overbeck and the Nazarenes. But while Romantic painters indulged in a sentimental nostalgia for the past that involved no innovations of form and kept rather to the balanced design of Neoclassicism, producing a pictorial equivalent of the serial story, Courbet and Daumier, and within certain limits the Barbizon landscapists Daubigny and Millet, were looking at nature with a fresh eye and trying to establish a deeper, more personal relationship with her. But their efforts met with no comprehension, except from an enlightened

middle-class minority (also regarded with suspicion on that account), who were subsequently joined by two or three courageous dealers. Painters and sculptors who failed to conform were systematically excluded from the official exhibitions and won no medals or prizes; this meant in effect that they could sell very few pictures. Such "nonconformists" as Baudelaire and Flaubert were actually brought into court. While the ostensible charge against them was that of an offense against public morals, their real crime in the eyes of their judges was that they had rebelled against the prevailing taste. The state, through the overseers of morals and conduct who represented it, was determined to impose and maintain its own aesthetic.

Altered social conditions and the rise of the bourgeoisie at the expense of the aristocracy had extended the scope of cultural activities, and there were now far more people interested in art than before the Revolution. Most of them, however, had no criteria of judgment or appreciation, and the established authorities used the press as a means of combating any tendency towards innovation. The press neither educated nor offered guidance, but catered for the most jejune and facile tastes.

The French Salons were among the most important public exhibitions of art; biennial through most of the eighteenth century, they were held annually after the Revolution, and there was never any lack of critics who were prompt to applaud the verdicts of the academic jury. When in 1866 Zola wrote his articles in praise of Manet in *L'Evénement*, the editor of the paper, alarmed at the letters of protest which they gave rise to, called him sharply to order and brought in an orthodox critic, one Pelloquet, whose first task it was to reassure the public and make it quite clear that he, Pelloquet, took a very different view of Manet.

The orthodox critics' systematic attacks first on the Realists, then on the Impressionists, Divisionists and Symbolists, forms a curious chapter of the history of taste, and also of social history. What did the public want? What should be the attitude of the new ruling class? Baudelaire addressed an appeal to the bourgeoisie, reminding them of their responsibility towards society and therefore towards culture: "You are the majority, both in numbers and intelligence; so you have the power, and can dispense justice." The middle classes were well-to-do, well-informed, it was their duty to enlighten others, to welcome beauty, to feel it. "Art," Baudelaire warned them, "is an infinitely precious possession," not to be scattered or squandered, and "to drop behind in art and politics is suicide."

Morris was far less optimistic about the cultural function of the middle classes. He accused them of being content with imitation, of caring only for excessive opulence and conceiving of art as "going hand in hand with luxury." His analysis of the way artistic production was conditioned by the values of a capitalist economy is most penetrating and he draws the right conclusions from it. "There is in the public of today no real knowledge of art, and little love for it. Nothing, save at the best certain vague prepossessions, which are but the phantom of that tradition which once bound artist and public together. Therefore the artists are obliged to express themselves, as it were, in a language not understood by the people. Nor is this their fault. If they were to try, as some think they should, to meet the public half-way and work in such a manner as to satisfy at any cost those vague prepossessions of men ignorant of art, they would be casting aside their special gifts, they would be traitors to the cause of art, which it is their duty and glory to serve."

The 1848 revolution revived the artists' hopes of obtaining more liberal exhibitions. The Salons were controlled by the state and that control was maintained until 1881; the fluctuations of French political life in that period were accordingly reflected in the greater or lesser liberality of the selection committees. But just as the political hopes of 1848 were soon dashed, so the liberality of the Salon juries was also short-lived. The effect of the *coup d'état* of 1851, the establishment of the Second Empire under Napoleon III, and the authoritarian powers given to Count Nieuwerkerke as head of the administration of the Beaux-Arts, was to impose a state-controlled aesthetic. Many changes for the worse brought about by the artistic policy of the Second Empire were to persist long after the fall of Napoleon III in 1870. All honors and awards were reserved for the official artists and academicians, members of the Institute; forming a solidly entrenched body backed by the government, they used their power ruthlessly to discriminate against any artist who showed the least originality. The government, in accordance with its avowed policy of restricting liberty and rights as much as possible, had to keep a strict control over art and justify itself in the eyes of the public, which in artistic matters was always ready to approve government policy. Art thus became an instrument used for demagogic purposes.

It is important to remember too that the 1848 uprising had been termed the "intellectuals' revolution," so that anything new or speculative in the field of thought and ideas was regarded with suspicion, and—it must be added—rightly so from the point of view of the established government. For it was in the nineteenth century that avant-garde art came to be identified, often if not always, with left-wing politics. This identification began with the Romantic writers and painters (though it was already true of David), and it continued even more noticeably with the Positivists and Realists, with Daumier and Courbet. It still persisted with the Impressionists, though among them were sincere reactionaries like Degas and bourgeois like Manet, whose political ideas were very different from those which informed, for example, Pissarro's anarchic socialism. In England, Morris was actively pledged to the socialist movement; in Italy, as Lionello Venturi has pointed out, the renewal brought about by the Macchiaioli began during the 1848 revolution and the wars of independence: "It was therefore of a revolutionary character, and what it most fervently aspired to was an artistic, spiritual and individual freedom corresponding to Italy's newly-won social and political freedom. It goes without saying that the men who had taken part in a revolution and a war, had been victorious, and were now devoting themselves to painting, brought to their art the ideals and aspirations for which they had fought." It is a significant fact that the radical press was on the whole more sympathetic to the new art trends. In Paris, in 1876, the conservative *Moniteur Universel* attacked the progressive paper *Le Rappel* for publishing an article by Emile Blémont on the Impressionists: "Let us take this opportunity of letting the 'impressionists' know that they have found favor in the eyes of *Le Rappel*. The radicals in art joining hands with the radicals in politics—that was only to be expected."

The concession in 1863 of a special "Salon des Refusés," as it was called, where the pictures rejected by the official Salon were exhibited, was an astute move on the part of Napoleon III. The adverse reaction of the public and the scandal caused by Manet's *Déjeuner sur l'herbe* decided the issue in favor of the academicians. This time the new art was condemned in the name of the people. The bourgeoisie that Baudelaire had appealed to was reluctant to run any risks; their standard of judgment was so-called common sense.

According to Charles Monselet, writing in *Le Figaro* under the pen-name of M. de Cupidon, Manet was "a pupil of Goya and Baudelaire" who had already made himself "repugnant to the bourgeoisie." For the public, wrote Zola in 1866, "a work of art, a picture, is only a pleasant thing that stirs the heart with gentle or awful sensations"; the crowd asks for nothing from the artist but "a tear or a smile." Tears and smiles came easily to those "apes of sentiment," the official painters and sculptors. Sentimentality did duty for the real feeling which, by now, most people could no longer recognize when they saw it and, what is worse, did not even miss. Everything was judged by shallow, literary conventions. "Emma longed to know the real meaning in life of the words *bliss*, *passion* and *rapture*, which had seemed so beautiful to her in books": in Emma Bovary Flaubert draws an admirable picture of the sentimental state of a woman of the petty bourgeoisie. Cézanne warned artists against "bookishness" and "intangible speculations," and maintained that, after so much tearful pathos, it was time to shout "Long live the sun that gives us such beautiful light!" But official art was against light and color, preferring dark, muddy tones. Couture's studio seemed to Manet like a tomb because "the light is false and the shadows are false." But the public was so used to dull tonalities that it turned away in dismay from any flash of light or color. Things were much the same in England until Morris took to bright colors, declaring that there were no such dark and dismal shades in nature as contemporary decorators seemed to delight in.

Unlike Courbet and the Realists who preceded them, the Impressionists were not concerned with the "social message" of art. But by claiming an absolute autonomy of expression, refusing to recognize the old hierarchy of genres or to imitate the past, and affirming the need for a sincere expression of real feeling, they ran directly counter to the sentimentality of middle-class taste. They were convinced that only a complete renewal of vision, a new way of seeing, could express the truth and reality of modern life, and not only in painting. *L'Impressionniste*, a short-lived paper launched in support of the new movement, printed in 1877 two letters on the state of architecture which were signed "A Painter," but which were in fact written by Renoir. Why, asked Renoir, was the new Louvre so ugly? "Because, I think, the decorations of the new Louvre are heavy, commonplace, done by workmen chosen at random, while the decorations of the old Louvre are light and the work of artists." And again he says, "Les Halles are the only buildings in Paris that have a genuinely original character and a style suited to their purpose." The great painter was thinking on almost the same lines as the great architects and engineers who were his contemporaries, thus showing that an art period always has an underlying cultural unity.

"The first revolution to be brought about," continued Renoir, "is the suppression of the Ecole des Beaux-Arts. Let the Conservatoire des Arts et Métiers be expanded so as to give young people the scientific grounding indispensable to the practice of their art. Let them be encouraged to strike out on their own, and above all let no one force them to copy the Old Masters, as is stupidly done today. No architect has ever yet departed from the path mapped out for him by the Ecole des Beaux-Arts. The Trinité, the Opéra, the Palais de Justice, the new Louvre, the Tribunal de Commerce, the Hôtel Dieu, are all Baroque, full of reminiscences of a style long since defunct. Gothic and Greek come together in strange marriages. For some years now sham Byzantine has been the dominant style of church architecture. Tomorrow it will be some other resurrection."

But of course such ideas brought the Impressionists into conflict with those middle-class convictions which were bound up with the very principles of a conservative society and the related belief that standards of artistic judgment had been laid down once and for all by the Academy. The so-called art lover "admires only the artist who corrupts by being himself corrupted." So wrote Telemaco Signorini, one of the leading nineteenth-century Italian painters, after visiting the 1873 Salon in Paris. He was forced however to the sad conclusion that taste was no better in any other country, and that "while at home we admire naked flesh discreetly veiled, here they admire the *Daphnis and Chloe* by Cabanel's pupil Morot." Signorini also felt that new means of pictorial expression might contribute to a change in the social order and regarded Degas's pictures as "elaborations of a new idea for a new society in the making, elements of a future art destined perhaps to break with all the traditions of the past and to bury in oblivion the vile practices of the present-day prostitution of art."

Official art was in fact an expression of the privileges of one class and its power of enslavement. It reflected the ascendancy of a bourgeoisie which, though devoid of critical insight, presumed to lay down the law in art and banish from its sight, with self-righteous airs of disgust and reprobation, anything that seemed to offend its sense of decorum. Such was the attitude, as late as 1898, of the Société des Gens de Lettres towards Rodin's *Balzac*. There is no better illustration of the philistinism of that day than the story of the Caillebotte bequest. Gustave Caillebotte was a naval engineer and a very fine amateur painter. He became friendly with the Impressionists, fell under their influence, took part in their exhibitions and bought their pictures. In a will made in 1883 he bequeathed his collection of sixty-seven paintings to the state. When he died in 1894, his brother and Renoir, as executors of the will, attempted to carry out its provisions. But the opposition was overwhelming; the protests of the Academy were so fierce and vociferous that the state, after protracted discussions, ruled that twenty-nine of the pictures must be refused—three by Cézanne, two by Manet, eight by Monet, eleven by Pissarro, two by Renoir and three by Sisley. At the urging of Caillebotte's brother, Vollard went to see Léonce Bénédite, curator of the Luxembourg Museum, and besought him to accept the rejected works, if only to store them away in the attic. "I?" replied Bénédite, "an official in whom the state has reposed its trust, receive pictures which the Commission has refused!"

The rebuffs suffered by the Impressionists—"the young artists without laurels," as Frédéric Chevalier called them in 1877—in their struggle for recognition are the most glaring example of the obstructive power of a bourgeoisie blindly opposed to works that are considered today to rank among the greatest ever produced by man. And the situation was no different in other parts of Europe. In 1869 Courbet wrote to Castagnary that real painting was unappreciated in Germany, that painters there were wholly preoccupied with the laws of perspective and the accuracy of historical costumes. Yet at the very conservative International Fine Arts Exhibition held in Munich in the same year Courbet was represented, and so were Millet, Decamps, Daubigny, Diaz, Théodore Rousseau, Corot and even Manet. At the 1892 exhibition of the Berlin Artists' Association, however, the hostility of the public was such that Munch was forced to withdraw his paintings. When the first Venice Biennale was held in 1895, it was described in the catalogue as "a soberly assessed collection of choice and original works"; but the advisory committee, which had the last word in deciding which artists were to be invited, included not only Puvis de Chavannes, Gustave Moreau, Millais, Burne-Jones and Max Liebermann, but the very men—Carolus-Duran, Boldini, Zorn—whose refined and trivial elegance was so dear to the bourgeoisie. In the circumstances the presence of Vittorio Pica, a critic who knew and appreciated the Impressionists, was unavailing, and it was not until 1920 that a Cézanne exhibition could at last be seen in Venice!

The truth is that by the end of the nineteenth century the official exhibitions had lost all contact with reality and no longer served any useful purpose. Having systematically excluded the men who were doing really original work, they were superseded by the activities of intelligent dealers like Durand-Ruel and Vollard, and by enthusiastic collectors like Hoschedé, Gustave Arosa, who was Gauguin's guardian, Count Doria, who in 1874 bought Cézanne's *Hanged Man's House*, and Dr Paul Gachet, most famous of all, in whose house at Auvers Van Gogh died in 1890. The artists themselves moreover banded together and organized exhibitions of their own. The first challenge issued to the public, in the name of an absolute faith in the rightness of their own ideas and works, was the exhibition of the Impressionists (or, as they then styled themselves, the "Société anonyme des Artistes peintres, sculpteurs et graveurs"), which opened in Paris on May 15, 1874, in the studios of the photographer Nadar at 35 Boulevard des Capucines. Seven more group exhibitions followed in 1876, 1877, 1878, 1880, 1881, 1882 and 1886. They met for the most part with hostility, ridicule or cold indifference, but they set a moral example which was followed by other artists. In 1884 were founded the Société des Vingt in Brussels and the Société des Indépendants in Paris. In 1890 Rodin, Puvis de Chavannes and Carrière founded the Société Nationale des Beaux-Arts and the first Salon de la Libre Esthétique was held in Brussels in 1896. The European avant-garde organized themselves in "secession" groups at Munich in 1892, Vienna in 1897, and Berlin in 1898, and these were important for the influence they exerted on all forms of artistic expression, not only painting and sculpture; above all, by imposing their style on the products of highly qualified craftsmen, they contributed to the international diffusion of Art Nouveau. In the United States a public free from traditional dogmas gave a warm reception to the Impressionist Exhibition organized by Durand-Ruel in New York in 1886. Exulting in the strength and power of persuasion which it drew from its adherence to the true course of history, the new art drove the "apes of sentiment" into the shades of oblivion.

NATURE: A COLLOQUY

One of the glories of French painting is its great landscape tradition, yet landscape was considered a minor genre by the nineteenth-century academics. For direct contact with nature made the aping of sentiments difficult, and their prejudice against open-air painting served to mask their inability to come to grips with nature. No forward-looking painter however but tried his hand at representing natural scenery. In landscape painting best of all we can trace the changes that came over the painter's idiom and his approach to the subject. By the second half of the nineteenth century painters had come to regard the sea, rivers and water in general not as picturesque or emotive elements but as terms of comparison enabling them to test and perfect a new way of seeing.

Many vanguard artists were attracted to the Channel coast of Normandy, to seaside towns like Honfleur and Trouville; there, between 1865 and 1867, Courbet, Jongkind, Daubigny, Boudin, Whistler and Monet were at work together. All of them studied light effects in the open air, sensitive and by no means passive observers of the ever-changing face of nature, with whom they established a colloquy, an exchange of impressions and reactions, of sensations and emotions. Here Courbet painted some of his most monumental seascapes, rendered in a thick impasto shot through with vibrant gleams of light. Even Daubigny brightened up his landscapes, throwing off the ponderosity of Barbizon realism and concentrating on those gradations of color which open form and allow it to be penetrated by the atmosphere. Boudin and Jongkind lightened their brushstroke and took to transparent colors; while neither ever actually became an Impressionist, both exerted an influence on Monet. Whistler, who in 1865 was on particularly friendly terms with Courbet, rendered natural scenery in paintings that already were faintly symbolic and reflect the decorative patterning of Oriental art.

For all these artists nature was a source of inspiration which enabled them to express themselves with the utmost sincerity. In front of nature the painter had to be himself, he could rely only on his own powers, tell only his own story and afford to disregard the pale abstractions conceived in the closed world of the studio. This was the period of thoroughgoing naturalism, whose limitations it was left to the Impressionists to overcome on the strength of a greater autonomy of vision. But this colloquy with nature, while contributing to liberate painters from set formulas of objective reproduction, also laid the basis for a new awareness of the moral implications of the artist's work.

GUSTAVE COURBET (1819-1877). SEASCAPE, 1866. WALLRAF-RICHARTZ MUSEUM, COLOGNE.

FRANÇOIS DAUBIGNY (1817-1878). VIEW ON THE SHORE. RIJKSMUSEUM, AMSTERDAM.

CLAUDE MONET (1840-1926). BEACH AT SAINTE-ADRESSE, 1867. THE ART INSTITUTE OF CHICAGO.

EUGÈNE BOUDIN (1824-1898). THE PIER AT TROUVILLE, 1869. THE BURRELL COLLECTION, GLASGOW ART GALLERY AND MUSEUM.

JOHANN BARTHOLD JONGKIND (1819-1891). BOATS ON THE SCHELDT, 1866. WATERCOLOR. LOUVRE, PARIS.

JAMES MCNEILL WHISTLER (1834-1903). HARMONY IN BLUE AND SILVER: TROUVILLE, 1865.
THE ISABELLA STEWART GARDNER MUSEUM, BOSTON.

can possibly succeed. I am convinced that the ill-applied improvements in photography have contributed largely, as have I think all purely material improvements, to the impoverishment of the French artistic genius, already so rare... It is obvious that industry, bursting in upon art, is fast becoming its deadliest enemy and that the confusion of functions is preventing any from being properly fulfilled."

Baudelaire's rather bitter remarks may seem a little excessive today, but they were based on a clear view of the actual facts. True, photographic techniques were on occasion turned to good account. Corot, for example, used them to make his *clichés-verre*. Coating a glass plate with a suitable substance, like albumen, he exposed it to the light in order to darken it; on this he incised his drawing which then, from this "negative," was printed on sensitized paper. But this was a purely graphic procedure; for the engraver's hand-press Corot substituted the glass plate and light-sensitive paper. Baudelaire hit the mark when he called photography the refuge of unsuccessful artists. (Yet this was not always the case: Degas practised photography for his own pleasure, and one of the best American painters of the nineteenth century, Thomas Eakins, was also a photographer.) Among those who gave up art for photography are O.G. Rejlander, H.P. Robinson, and Mathew Brady. No wonder then that many photographers conformed to the worst standards of contemporary painting. Thus Rejlander, in *The Two Ways of Life*, produced an elaborate composition in the manner of certain painters of the day who incongruously grouped together imaginary figures decked out in historical costumes. The complicated and exacting methods Rejlander employed to make this photograph were worthy of a better cause and better taste: the final picture was the result of thirty different negatives combined with wonderful ingenuity. Robinson did the same. His *Fading Away* was obtained from a combination of five negatives, but the result was no better than a third-rate painting. Julia Margaret Cameron followed suit, attracted by the literary sentimentalism of the English painter G.F. Watts, who was not only her source of inspiration but her actual model for *The Kiss of Peace*.

CAMILLE COROT (1796-1875).
DANTE AND VIRGIL, 1858. CLICHÉ-VERRE.
KUNSTMUSEUM, BERN.

OSCAR G. REJLANDER (1813-1875).
THE TWO WAYS OF LIFE, 1857.
COLLECTION OF THE
ROYAL PHOTOGRAPHIC SOCIETY, LONDON.
▼

NADAR (1820-1910).
SARAH BERNHARDT, 1859.
BIBLIOTHÈQUE NATIONALE, PARIS.

HENRY PEACH ROBINSON (1830-1910).
FADING AWAY, 1858. COMBINATION PRINT.
COLLECTION OF THE
GEORGE EASTMAN HOUSE, ROCHESTER, N.Y.
▼

2

PHOTOGRAPHY

One might suppose that when photography first appeared it was used chiefly with a view to giving an exact and immediate picture of the visible world. While in some cases this was true, in many others the long exposure time required to fix the image on the photographic plate led to a certain elaboration and, very often, an arbitrary idealization of that image. This might have been all to the good if photography, used as an art in its own right, had proved capable of the necessary autonomy of expression. But there could be no autonomy when its imagery was simply taken over from the most pedestrian type of contemporary painting. The general public, despising Courbet and all the painters who failed to give them an idealized picture of reality, expected photographers merely to provide equivalents of the feeble pictures which they appreciated—with the result that photography, instead of improving taste, merely helped to degrade it.

Baudelaire, in his review of the 1859 Salon, commented on this state of affairs. "As the photographic industry," he wrote, "became the refuge of all the painters who were unsuccessful, ill-qualified or too lazy to complete their training, the camera craze took on not only a character of blindness and imbecility but a color of revenge. I do not believe, I cannot believe, that so stupid a conspiracy in which, as in all conspiracies, wretches and dupes are involved,

JULIA MARGARET CAMERON (1815-1879). THE KISS OF PEACE: THE PAINTER G. F. WATTS AND HIS CHILDREN, ABOUT 1867. A. L. COBURN COLLECTION, RHOS-ON-SEA, NORTH WALES.

MATHEW B. BRADY (1823-1896). RUINS OF THE GALLEGO FLOUR MILLS AT RICHMOND, VA., 1865.
COLLECTION THE MUSEUM OF MODERN ART, NEW YORK.

EADWEARD MUYBRIDGE (1830-1904). HORSE IN MOTION, 1878.
COLLECTION OF THE GEORGE EASTMAN HOUSE, ROCHESTER, N.Y.

It is perhaps unfair to pass judgment on these incunabula of a new art. But one thing is certain: their influence on the taste of the public, as Baudelaire saw, was deplorable. They are interesting nevertheless as showing the stages of photography's progress towards its own autonomy of expression. Robinson was interested in soft-focus effects and published a book on the subject; he was concerned, not with photographic technique as an end in itself, but with working out a style of pictorial photography. Mrs Cameron's pictures too are out of focus, but the effects thus obtained are in her case not so much intentional as owing to the fact that the large plates she used were ill-adapted to the focal length of the lens.

These reserves do not apply to Nadar. A radical both in life and art, a friend of the Impressionists to whom he lent his studio for their first group exhibition, the photographer who supplied Ingres with photographs for his portraits, an engraver and colleague of Daumier, Nadar produced portrait photographs in which the image, modeled by light with strong contrasts, at last acquires its full autonomy. Perhaps his boldest innovation was his aerial views of Paris taken from a balloon. Then there were those who, despite the limitations imposed by the cameras of a hundred years ago, set out to chronicle current events; this was to become one of the major roles of photography. The English photographer Fenton covered the Crimean War, and Mathew Brady the American Civil War; Brady, following the troops into battle, produced the first photographs of war dead and ruined cities.

Eadweard Muybridge made some of the earliest action photographs in 1872. His experiments were carried out at the request of a horse lover who had laid a wager that a trotting horse, at a given moment, has all four hoofs off the ground. Muybridge's photographs proved this to be true. He also analyzed human movements and thereby—though without intending it—called into question the conventional representations of academic painters, who from now on were well advised to consult Muybridge's photograms in order to avoid blunders in their rendering of human beings in action.

II

A NEW ORDER

THE SETTING OF MODERN LIFE

Urban growth is the characteristic feature of modern community life as it has developed since the end of the Renaissance. This trend neither began nor ended in the nineteenth century, but it was then that it first assumed gigantic and abnormal proportions. In the first fifty years of the nineteenth century the population of London and Paris doubled. The numerical relation between countryfolk and city dwellers was everywhere rapidly changing. Industry being concentrated in the urban centers, country people were drawn citywards, in ever larger numbers, in search of new jobs and a higher standard of living. The existing urban structures, medieval, Renaissance or Baroque, were unable to cope with this expanding population, nor were working conditions in the factory in any way comparable with those of the craftsman's workshop. An altogether different setting was called for, but population and production went on increasing with none of the order of an organic process. The overcrowding of cities, the speculation and rise of land values caused by uncontrolled expansion, the lack of social and sanitary legislation, the failure to make any provision for future needs—all this created a situation unprecedented in history and quite abnormal. If to this is added the resulting estrangement of man from the natural surroundings to which he is physically adapted, from what biologists call the biosphere, then it is clear that the urgent need to improve conditions of city life involved problems of vital importance for the survival of man and society. Town planning is more than a technique, it is a social science.

"Industrialism, the main creative force of the nineteenth century, produced the most degraded urban environment the world had yet seen; for even the quarters of the ruling classes were befouled and overcrowded" (Lewis Mumford). Something has been said of William Morris's reaction to all this and his active efforts to improve living conditions. But the situation was such that town planning had not only been far outstripped by the techniques of industrial production; it was compelled in practice to face problems which had never before arisen and to solve them not in opposition to but in harmony with changed conditions. This endeavor achieved some measure of success in the most advanced countries, but it did not go forward without conflicts and contradictions.

The prevailing ideology, protected by law, was that of capitalism and free enterprise; the inviolability of private property was its fundamental principle. Even planners who belonged to the conservative upper class, like Baron Haussmann in Paris, were frustrated when they attempted to appropriate privately owned land for public use. This idea of the sanctity of private property became a target for the criticism of sociologists from Proudhon to Marx and Engels, and of writers of the most varied outlook, not only European but also American. Hawthorne, in *The House of the Seven Gables*, published in 1851, puts these words in the mouth of one of the characters: "What we call real estate—the solid ground to build a house on—is the broad foundation on which nearly all the guilt of the world rests. A man will commit almost any wrong—he will heap up an immense pile of wickedness, as hard as granite and which will weigh as heavily on his soul, to eternal ages—only to build a great, gloomy, dark-chambered mansion, for himself to die in, and for his posterity to be miserable in . . . Within the lifetime of the child already born . . . all this will be done away with. The world is growing too ethereal and spiritual to bear these enormities a great while longer."

The cultural plea for change which we find even in Dickens and many other writers was altered to a moral imperative, and over and above the concern with social, economic and hygienic improvement, ethical principles went to shape the ideology of the new town planners and changed their technical assumptions. It should be noted moreover that from the first reforms of the Utopians to the idea of the garden city (i.e. from Robert Owen to Ebenezer Howard) the concern of town planners was to provide the basic structures not for *any* society helplessly exposed to the irresistible pressures of technology and capital, but for a democratic society in which each and all, from entrepreneur to worker, should have their place, their rights, and the homes and environment essential to health and happiness. The town planner, in his effort to meet actual needs, was thus led to look with a critical eye on existing institutions. Urban reform however was in fact initiated by conservative leaders. The first health laws, laying down the minimum hygienic requirements for dwelling houses and taking measures against water pollution, were passed as a result of the cholera epidemics that occurred in France and England after 1830. Subsidized housing legislation and the building of workers' communities, like those of Krupp at Essen, had utilitarian or paternalistic motives. The replanning of Paris, resolved on by Napoleon III and carried out by Baron Haussmann, was the first great transformation of a modern city and it too was motivated in part by reasons of public utility.

Here were concrete results and they helped to improve squalid living conditions which had been denounced by progressive Catholics, like the Société de Saint-Vincent-de-Paul in France, or by Socialists. Nevertheless, nineteenth-century town planning was handicapped by the conservative spirit behind it; its shortcomings were due to the lack of any unity of vision or policy in the organization of urban space, the feebleness of government attempts to expropriate land in the public interest, and the excessive freedom given to private speculators who had soon learned how to turn the new housing regulations to their own advantage.

By mid-century the existing tradition, still a very young one, was that of the Utopians, the first who sought, in theory and occasionally in practice, to impose order on the space necessary for life and work in a radically changed environment: Robert Owen in England, Charles Fourier and Etienne Cabet in France. As early as 1817 Owen, a cotton manufacturer who felt it his duty to resolve the conflict between human labor and machinery, proposed a plan for working communities which

he developed more fully in 1820. Each community was to form a self-sufficing township based on a cooperative economy, with a population of from 300 to 2000, the optimum number being 800 to 1200. The township was to be laid out on strictly geometric lines around a central square or parallelogram, with various buildings on each side: private dwellings, children's dormitories, infirmary, hostel and storehouses. Along the central axis of the parallelogram, so spaced out as to allow for plenty of air and light, were the church, public kitchens and mess-rooms. The community had its own land to cultivate. Its internal economy was based on the value of labor; its relation to the state remained unchanged, members of the community continuing to pay taxes and do military service. But all this required a heavy outlay of capital, and this was the weak point of the scheme. Owen could find no one in Europe to finance it. In 1825, looking now to America, Owen himself purchased the village of Harmony in Indiana, which he renamed New Harmony. There he attempted to put his ideas into practice. The experiment lasted till 1828; by then it was an admitted failure and Owen returned to England. His ideas greatly influenced the English cooperative movement and the formation of trade unions. As regards town planning, though other communities followed the principles he laid down, Owen's notions of harmony and cooperation seemed for the time being to offer no solution to the problem. They did show, however, that that problem could only be solved within the context of social and political realities, as distinct from abstract technical considerations.

Charles Fourier in France, even before Ruskin, dreamed of a reorganization of society which would enable each to obtain personal satisfaction from his work, a well-organized industrial society in which private interests would be subordinated to that end. At first he imagined an ideal city built up around a central nucleus and spreading outwards in concentric zones. Houses in the city itself were to be surrounded by green spaces at least equal in extent to the built-up area; in the outer zones, where factories and suburbs were located, the green belt was to be more extensive. This orderly arrangement contrasted with the congestion, squalor and chaos of the industrial city as it actually was, but in Fourier's eyes that arrangement was but a transitional step towards the next phase of his social Utopia, that of supreme harmony as realized in the "phalanx" and "phalanstery." The phalanx was a model community numbering 1620 members, the phalanstery a common building designed to house them all and laid out with an order and equilibrium very much in the Neoclassical style. The phalanstery formed a residential unit in which the whole life of the community was lived, and its plan was worked out in elaborate detail. There were many attempts to realize Fourier's ideals, not only in France but in Algeria, New Caledonia and the United States. An agricultural community inspired by those ideals was founded by George Ripley at West Roxbury, Massachusetts, in 1841: this was Brook Farm, of which Hawthorne was a member for a time, and which attracted the attention of Emerson and many other prominent Americans. But all these experiments were short-lived, all ended in failure. Only the "Familistère" of Jean-Baptiste Godin, a community settlement at Guise in northern France where Fourier's ideas were adopted in a modified form, has lasted down to the present day.

While Owen and Fourier visualized small communities, Etienne Cabet, in his novel *Voyage en Icarie* published in Paris in 1840, imagined a large city designed on a geometric plan, divided into sixty districts and traversed by a river; the distribution of space and circulation of traffic were carefully regulated. Icaria was to be a metropolis with a collective, communistic, internationalist economy and its architecture was to be eclectic, representing various national styles. The community Cabet actually founded, in America, was very different and was doomed to failure by internal dissensions and practical difficulties. In 1847 he launched a manifesto entitled *Allons en Icarie* and announced that he had acquired some land in Texas. The next year a group of his followers sailed to the United States, but the land was too much divided up to be used for the kind of community life which the Icarians proposed to lead. Cabet went out in person to America in 1849, but by then the group was on the move. They went first to New Orleans, then to Cheltenham, near St Louis, and finally, after a quarrel which reduced their numbers, settled at Corning, Iowa, in 1860. (Cabet himself died at St Louis in 1856.) Further dissensions in 1876 split the little community into two factions, the Young Party and the Old Party. The latter founded New Icaria a short distance from the old settlement; the Young Party migrated to the vicinity of Cloverdale, Sonoma County, California,

and established the Icaria-Speranza Community. Neither of the two experiments lasted till the end of the century, and as only a few hundred persons participated in them both communities were quite the reverse of the communistic metropolis visualized by Cabet.

The searching criticism of the scientific socialists, of Marx and Engels in particular, continued to develop in spite of the failure of these utopian enterprises; indeed it was hostile to them from the start. The problem that had been raised, the reorganization of living space in order to strike a balance between the needs of the workers and the requirements of production, was capable of other solutions and it led in particular to the planning of workers' cities and to Ebenezer Howard's garden city. But nineteenth-century town planners were not starry-eyed Utopians, they realized that some of the problems confronting them called for an immediate solution. Their most conspicuous efforts, if not always their best, were made in the big cities, which were being transformed by the Industrial Revolution. They were no longer adapted to modern life; overcrowded and unhealthy, they lacked the open space, means of transport, stations, shops and markets required by an ever-growing number of consumers; above all, they lacked the sanitary arrangements which offered the only sure defense against disease and epidemics.

Between 1853 and 1869 Haussmann transformed Paris. He extended the metropolis to include new suburbs, and at the same time decentralized the administration, put through new thoroughfares, long, broad and straight, and provided for green spaces and public parks. He created the Paris we see today. To do this he had to use high-handed methods and was able to do so as he derived his authority directly from the emperor. He was bitterly opposed by the Liberals, who rose up in defense of free enterprise and private property, and also by the working class; he was attacked by the legislature and ordered to restore to its owners the land he had appropriated around the streets he was opening up—land which, because of those new streets, had enormously increased in value. He offended not only economic interests, but traditional and cultural ones as well. But he set an example of urban transformation based on careful planning and fruitful collaboration between technicians and administrators.

Technical and economic aims, however, were all too often considered in the abstract and pursued for their own sake. Haussmann allowed the historic center of Paris to be gutted; in this too his example was followed and the wanton demolition of historic buildings has become one of the saddest features of our own century. He did not see that a city is kept alive in the architectural memorials of its past. These have grown up in response to human needs, and by ignoring them, as Haussmann did, man's place in the urban setting is diminished and rendered artificial. His conception of the city was monumental, scenographic, Baroque; the city, for him, was the outward embodiment of a power that claimed to be absolute and still acted according to the laws of persuasion. "In some ways," as Bruno Zevi has said, "Haussmann tackled modern problems; he provided for the flow of traffic and thought of the city as a machine. But in his psychological and moral attitude, he was the last artificer of an aristocratic and grandiloquent age that was about to pass away." And indeed the moral factor, as we have already pointed out, is of cardinal importance in the renewal of an urban culture. It is worth noting—though we must not infer too much from it—that at this very time, in the 1860s and especially in the years after the fall of the Second Empire, the impressionist conception of space was squarely opposed to Haussmann's. Impressionist space is not defined *a priori*, it is not immutable, but embraces all human experience that can be enacted within it; it is a space in which the traditional, demonstrative monumentality no longer has any *raison d'être*.

Following the example of Paris, and under pressure of dire necessity, many European cities embarked on re-urbanization programs, each bent on resolving its own particular problems—Barcelona, Brussels, Vienna, Florence, and finally Berlage's plan for Amsterdam in 1902. Workers' communities were founded too, like Saltaire in Yorkshire in 1853 and the *cité ouvrière* at Mulhouse in Alsace. Urban legislation became more efficient, and laws were passed like the Housing of the Working Classes Act in England in 1890. Nineteenth-century town planning arrived at two solutions of note: Ebenezer Howard's garden city and Tony Garnier's plan for an industrial city drawn up in 1901 and put forward in 1904. Mention should also be made of the theoretical work of the Austrian architect Camillo Sitte, which was published in 1899 under the title of *Der Städtebau nach seinen künstlerischen Grundsätzen*. It was based on the author's knowledge of the best features of the medieval town. Sitte believed that from those features a remedy could be derived for the improvement of modern cities, one which would replace abstract symmetry and exaggerated spaces with a historical vision of the problem—a vision which, as outlined by Sitte, came as a fitting and coherent conclusion to the nineteenth-century approach to town planning and pointed the way to new conceptions, if not to new solutions.

The problem of green spaces was given much thought, and not only for hygienic reasons. It was, for example, one of the positive aspects of Haussmann's planning. In London Bedford Park was laid out by Norman Shaw in 1875. In England this problem was taken seriously: Ruskin and Morris proclaimed the necessity of maintaining contact with nature, following in this an English tradition of long standing. Ruskin himself tried to establish a village in the country near Oxford in 1871; in 1887 Lever, an industrialist who admired his ideas, built six hundred houses surrounded by green spaces for the workers in his factory at Port Sunlight, near Liverpool. Another industrialist, Cadbury, repeated the experiment on a larger scale at Bournville near Birmingham in 1895. As for Ebenezer Howard, though his ideas were very close to those of the Utopians and William Morris, he showed a keen sense of the practical in his plans for a garden city. For him urban development was not a phenomenon that concerned the city alone; it had serious repercussions in the countryside, which it scarred and blighted. Unless controlled and directed, it ran counter to the laws of economic equilibrium and biological needs. Moreover, the problem of urban improvement had to be considered in all its ramifications throughout the area involved. If the worker employed in the city requires adequate housing, so does the man who tills the soil in the countryside. Howard's social imagination was far more searching and comprehensive than that of the thinkers who had concerned themselves only with the industrial working masses. He planned his garden city in terms of a maximum population of 32,000; the city included factories and was surrounded by an agricultural belt; houses were set well apart from each other and undisturbed by main-road traffic. He visualized a built-up area of about a thousand acres; around this urban nucleus extended a peripheral zone of some six thousand acres earmarked for cultivation and agricultural activities. These ideas, set forth in Howard's book *Tomorrow, A Peaceful Path to Real Reform*, published in 1898, were put into practice in England at Letchworth, designed by Barry Parker and Raymond Unwin in 1902, and Welwyn, designed by Louis de Soissons in 1919.

Tony Garnier's plan for an industrial city was certainly not a garden city, but it did not contradict it in principle. His urban nucleus was also planned for a population of about 35,000, with an inviolable green belt. Above all it had the merit of a highly rational distribution of space and architecture. Never lapsing into eclecticism, Garnier made the best possible use of modern materials like glass, iron and reinforced concrete. He saw architecture and town planning for what they were: inseparable aspects of the same problem. In a city like the one he planned, "each architectonic element," he said,

"has its rightful place and application." Open spaces are governed and proportioned by the buildings, and the position of each of these varies according to its function: the factory stands in the open plain, separated from the city by the railway; on high ground are hospital buildings, shielded from the wind and facing south; each sphere of life was given its appropriate setting. Garnier was the first architect to bring a rational vision to bear on the planning of a modern city. Heir to the great French tradition of rationalism, he applied its principles to the problems of urban development. Later he joined forces with Edouard Herriot, mayor of Lyons, who enabled him to realize his projects. Collaboration between a left-wing politician and an architect who was also a town planner and sociologist proved to be the most effective means of improving the conditions of modern city life. Such improvement was the highest aspiration of nineteenth-century town planners and their finest legacy to the century that followed.

THE PATH OF REASON

In his book *Art et Technique* Pierre Francastel quotes a remark of Henry van de Velde, the Belgian architect who was one of the initiators of Art Nouveau. It throws light on one of the most important and most contradictory aspects of nineteenth-century architecture: "The beauty of engineering results from the fact that the engineer is not conscious of any quest for beauty."

Like most judgments thrown off in the heat of a controversy such as Van de Velde found himself engaged in at the turn of the century, this one contains an element of truth and an element of error. It nevertheless testifies to the antithesis which the nineteenth-century believed to exist between the work of the architect and that of the engineer. For the latter was regarded as a pure functionalist and was credited with creating quite unconsciously, through his concentration on function, a new beauty corresponding to the perfect adaptation of form to purpose. But functionalism is no modern invention; this concept is as old as the world and the contrast drawn between architect and engineer is accordingly quite false. Already in the treatise of Vitruvius, which sums up the views on architecture of the ancient Greeks and Romans, no contrast is drawn between *distributio* (i.e. the suitability of the structural arrangement) and the *decorum* which results from the appearance of the building once it is finished in all its parts; the two coincide when the builder's art is based on *ratiocinatio* (i.e. knowledge of the laws of mathematical proportions). The technique of Baroque architects like Borromini or Guarino Guarini is conditioned, it is true, by the desire to achieve demonstrative and even spectacular effects, but this does not make it any less functional. Indeed, emboldened by that very technique, architects were able to design buildings that reflected a new outlook, which in turn gave rise to a new beauty. The contradiction between beauty and function occurs when architects compromise the autonomy of their own means of expression, when

decorum is understood as a mere superimposing of decorative elements or as an intermingling with other means of expression.

What was emphasized in the case of town planning also holds good for architecture: it cannot be considered as an abstract technique. Like every art it has various components and technical perfection alone is not enough to guarantee good results. By definition of course architecture is the science of building. The correspondence between science and technique (or better between scientific principles and technical applications) which once held good, and was still true of the Baroque period, which was directly influenced on the theoretical plane by Galileo's experimental methods—that correspondence, at some point in the course of the Industrial Revolution, ceased to hold good. Technique was put to the service of scientific research, and while the latter was still governed by the logic of things and events, it substituted its own pragmatic outlook for the ideology of science and ceased to attach any importance to the world-view and the will to moral progress which underlie the very principles of scientific research. In a word, technology destroyed the human dimensions of science. So it is that nineteenth-century culture, being still fundamentally humanistic, and rational to excess, regarded the engineer as a mere technician and denied him any capacity for artistic creation. For César Daly, for example, who in France was one of the champions of eclecticism in architectural design, the engineer was called upon to satisfy material needs, and these alone; it was for the architect to satisfy those of the spirit; the first acted in accordance with reason, the second with feeling.

This antithesis between two professions thought to be quite unconnected was obviously a legacy of Romanticism. Actually the differences between engineer and architect cancel each other out when the former is not only a technician and the latter is not a decorator. Their paths cross and even coincide when they attempt to renew the style of architectonic design, to restore its autonomy of expression and its contemporaneity. Then both together pursue what Viollet-le-Duc called the "path of reason," which leads them to a twofold result: the adaptation of technique to function and, in consequence, the discovery of a new dimension of beauty far removed from the codifications and contaminations of academic taste. In 1863 Anatole de Baudot declared that the architect is above any canon of beauty. A pupil of Labrouste and Viollet-le-Duc who later used reinforced concrete in building the church of Saint-Jean de Montmartre, Baudot took an active part in the debate over architectural design, his lectures and writings covering the latter half of the nineteenth century and the first decades of the twentieth. In his *Architecture, le passé, le présent*, in which about 1914 he summed up his ideas and experience, he ascribed the difficulties encountered by modern architecture in its search for a style and language of its own to the fact that "the new materials and processes, like iron and reinforced concrete, are ignominiously concealed, on the plea that they have an unsightly appearance."

The materials taken up by engineers and architects in the nineteenth century, with the exception of reinforced concrete and steel, both of which appeared later, were materials which industry had indeed made cheaper and more abundant, but which had been available and widely used in the past. They themselves were not new, they were simply put to new uses, incorporated in new structures, when builders began to realize that "form follows function" and that the material thus employed offers other possibilities, brings about a different dynamism, allows of a different distribution of masses and thrusts, with all that this implies on both the structural and stylistic plane. The antithesis then was not entirely between a new technique and the technique of the past, but rather between the latter and a working method which made a wider and fuller use of certain materials on the basis of increased scientific knowledge and different ideological premises. And since these premises call for a new approach to form and design, technique itself accordingly undergoes a change, a process of continual elaboration. Thus, as Pierre Francastel has put it, "the architecture of the nineteenth century begins to give us a remarkable example of

a technique employed to satisfy needs created by another knowledge, another set of tools, another way of life." The century's architecture began to take form, that is, when technique was subordinated to it, and not vice versa.

We should therefore be on our guard against any merely technical interpretation of the origins of modern architecture. As in the case of town planning (and in effect the two flow together and merge in the manner demonstrated by Tony Garnier's "industrial city"), the causes of renewal were not technical or economic, not social or moral, but all these together; that renewal came in response to a new cultural situation. The technological developments of the nineteenth century must be seen against a highly complex background, against implications of every kind. The growth of population, the need for new housing and services, expanding means of communication and transport, these were changing the human condition, changing men's outlook and above all increasing their power to change their environment. A nineteenth-century bridge obviously represents a technical achievement in which metal girders take the place of the traditional wood or stone, but it is also the product of science—not only the science of bridge building but of town planning and communications in which economic and social factors must be taken into account. All this is not enough to make it a work of art; it becomes one when, by the development of form and the fresh solution of structural problems, it goes to define an architectonic space. Architecture then becomes a reality of history and not a contingent moment in the annals of technology. Eiffel was undoubtedly an artist, and there is little point in trying to decide whether the man was an engineer or an architect when he exploited new techniques to open up new fields of knowledge, as he did in building his bridge over the Douro; even less point when he impaired his architectural style with decorative trimmings, as he did in the Eiffel Tower. For he attained to the level of artistic creation when he overcame the antithesis between reason and feeling; when he gives way to feeling in order to cater for a taste that is not his own, the result is negative, or anyhow not completely positive.

The avant-garde architects of the nineteenth century were trying to find their way back to rational procedures. Neo-Gothic was an attempt to meet

69

the demands of the modern sensibility by way of the structural audacities of medieval Gothic; this reversion to the past was not motivated merely by sentiment or attachment to tradition. Neoclassical design too, beginning with the early functionalism of Durand at the Ecole Polytechnique in Paris, was concerned with a rational organization of space, though differently conceived, and an adaptation of style to the needs of modern life. The strictures passed on neo-Gothic by the Ecole des Beaux-Arts in 1846, as recorded in the report of Raoul Rochelle, are based in part on grounds that can hardly be impugned. True, the conventional canons of beauty are here taken for granted, and judged by these canons neo-Gothic architecture seemed uncouth and inartistic in its absence of any system of proportions and any relation between masses and details. But there were other and more telling grounds for disapproval. "The question is," reads the report, "whether in a country like ours, in the midst of a civilization that no longer has anything of the Middle Ages, it is fitting and proper, or even possible, to build churches which would come as an oddity, an anachronism, a freak; which would look like an accident in the context of a whole new society, for they could never pretend to pass for a relic of a defunct society; which would form a glaring contrast to all that might be built or done around them and by this discrepancy alone would offend against reason, taste and religious sentiment."

There would be nothing to be said against this if the Ecole des Beaux-Arts had offered some alternative other than Neoclassicism, if in other words it had not been what it was—the stronghold of the most hidebound academicism and traditionalism in defiance of innovation of any kind. Even so, a few of those Neoclassical architects, like Durand at the beginning of the century or Guadet towards the end, helped to do away with some of the more objectionable features of architectural decoration. A historian of modern architecture, Luciano Benevolo, has pointed out that the designs contained in Durand's course of lectures, as published in 1826, "anticipate all the works carried out by the engineers of the nineteenth century. All the features of their work are clearly set forth: the approach to mechanical problems, the independence of the structural device with respect to the finishing of its elements, the predilection for estimates in round figures, and for elementary forms which reduce the designer's quirks to a

minimum. These features reappear in the works of Paxton, Eiffel, Contamin, Jenney and Hennebique." It is evident, nevertheless, that the Neoclassical style was ill adapted to the use of new materials which, with their higher resistance, reduced the extent of masses and surfaces.

As for neo-Gothic architecture, it was of course not a product of the nineteenth century but had its origins in the Gothic Revival of eighteenth-century England, in the writings of men like Hughes, Horace Walpole, Hurd and historians of architecture like Bentham and Willis. In the nineteenth century it found its natural and logical development in the Romantic nostalgia for the past, in the revaluation which the Romantics made of the Middle Ages—a time, it was realized, when art was capable of expressing collectively the practical, moral and religious needs of the community. Neo-Gothic had indeed great merits, over and above those vaunted by Ruskin and Morris. It brought about a renewal of architectural design, and contributed to the new approach to structural problems advocated by Viollet-le-Duc. It was a renewal that ignored sentimental affinities and proceeded resolutely along the "path of reason," and from a careful study of medieval monuments, viewed as a whole complex of structural and expressive values, it was impelled to take bold steps of its own, upheld by the use of modern materials, first iron or cast iron, then reinforced concrete. For the neo-Gothic architect an edifice was not a self-enclosed mass but a continuous articulation of volumes, of thrusts and counterthrusts, a succession of variously defined spatial units. And this view, the outcome of a deeper knowledge of ancient architecture, was handed down to the architects and engineers of the nineteenth century. A neo-Gothic edifice, moreover, seeks to establish a relation with nature, and it is not surprising that a culture favorable to such a style should have given rise to some outstanding examples of urban reorganization. Another of its distinctive features was its insistence on sincerity. With Pugin, even before Ruskin, appears the idea that art must have a moral basis, and this moral imperative demands of the artist an absolute sincerity of expression, such—in the case of the architect—as forbids him to conceal the structure of his building. Ruskin disliked metal and modern materials generally, but he disliked concealment even more; his *Seven Lamps of Architecture* includes the "lamp of truth." Baudot, as noted above, took the same view, not out of moral considerations, but in defense of a new standard of aesthetic values.

The use of materials supplied by the iron and steel industry in shapes and sizes differing from those of the past, and from those employed by craftsmen, took place of course in a cultural atmosphere which gave scope at times for other, even exotic manifestations; witness the orientalizing Royal Pavilion built by John Nash at Brighton in 1818. But these materials, with their increased resistance and the thinness of their sections, offered possibilities which inevitably represented a challenge to the repertory of traditional forms. Obviously, to take but one example, a cast-iron column could not act merely as a substitute for a marble column. In the United States James Bogardus proposed to emulate ancient architecture in his use of cast iron, but already in the Harper Building in New York, which he designed in 1854, the formal pattern determined by cast-iron columns visible externally marks a departure from traditional models. Moreover buildings had now to answer new purposes. Paxton had begun by designing conservatories, but the Crystal Palace was designed to house a great international exhibition and the result was a type of building such as had never been seen before. In this case Paxton's previous technical experience was a decisive factor, especially in the design of the prefabricated elements that went into the building, but technique was not an end in itself. Bridges, railway stations, markets like the Halles Centrales in Paris designed by Baltard in 1853, and great stores like the Bon Marché in Paris designed by Eiffel and Boileau in 1876, answered new demands; it would have been the height of folly to build them in the monumental styles of the past. The Galerie des Machines designed by Dutert and Contamin for the Paris World's Fair of 1889, while it kept to proportional relationships of the traditional type, was yet one of the masterpieces of nineteenth-century architecture (it was pulled down in 1910): its novelty lay not only in the use of metal structures, in the interplay of thrusts calculated to relieve the stress on articulated joints and on the light and sturdy piers, but in the new spatial conception of the great span which metal, thus employed, enabled architects to achieve. On the moving bridges crossing the great hall the public undoubtedly felt at ease within a space that surrounded it like a well-cut garment perfectly suited to the ceremony taking place.

It is hard to believe that all this was the result of a process unconsciously pursued, the more so as in the Galerie des Machines we find an architect, Dutert, joining forces with an engineer, Contamin —two men of different backgrounds and training working together smoothly. They could hardly have been conscious *a priori* of the beauty of their design, for it conformed to none of the canons then commonly accepted; their aim after all was to erect a "hall of machinery," something for which there were no traditional models and only a few very recent precedents. But true expression is attained only when the artist has a precise purpose in mind. The Eiffel Tower, to take another example, may be a less successful work, but it is hardly to be supposed that Eiffel and his assistants did not attempt to attain certain aesthetic values. The truth is that the historical significance of nineteenth-century architecture, the lesson it offered to the future, lies in its conscious effort to find a style uncontaminated by eclecticism and imitation, a style availing itself of the elements provided by the new technology, and elaborating those elements, not merely being dominated by them. Over and above contingent contradictions, this was the meaning behind the appeal to reason.

NEW MATERIALS

Ideas of decoration were transformed by the introduction first of metal structures, then of reinforced concrete. The engineers and architects who took them up were concerned to resolve them into appropriate forms without distorting their function. Metal was so flexible a material that, as James Bogardus maintained, it could be adapted to any style, whether Gothic or Renaissance. But the problem was not an easy one to deal with, for the new materials altered the nature and relationships of traditional design. Ruskin, though he detested metal, made no objection to it when it was used by Woodward and Deane in the 1850s to build the University Museum at Oxford, intended to house scientific and natural history collections; for this undertaking Ruskin himself acted as architectural supervisor. The main hall is designed like the nave of a Gothic cathedral; its slender, clustered columns convey a curiously naturalistic impression and indeed appear to have been inspired by plant forms. Ruskin's respect for truth was so great that there was no attempt to conceal the structure and materials of the building, whose only embellishment consisted of decorations added to the outer side of the arches, whose upward thrust emphasizes the verticalism of the design.

The Bibliothèque Impériale, as it was then called (now Bibliothèque Nationale), which Labrouste began erecting in Paris in 1855, represents a considerable improvement over the Bibliothèque Sainte-Geneviève of a few years before. Internally the problem of decoration has been successfully solved, the decorative elements not being superadded but forming an integral part of the metal arches. The interior space is not a single longitudinal unit, like that of a cathedral, but is diversified by the piers and the rhythmic pattern of the vaulted ceiling. Not a single element is based on natural forms, and the structure achieves a fine simplicity of design without any suggestion of eclecticism.

Metal structures—to the dismay of many who were still prejudiced against them—were now beginning to be used even in churches, as in Saint-Eugène in Paris, designed by Louis-Auguste Boileau in 1854-1855. When reinforced concrete was introduced, Hennebique took it up in France and exploited its resources to the full. It was used by Anatole de Baudot in the church of Saint-Jean de Montmartre, begun in 1894, despite the protests of a congregation that expected to see the building collapse upon them at any moment. The basic style employed was still Gothic, but Baudot gave it a new look by his skillful handling of the new techniques; the result is a wonderful lightness of structure and a rational distribution of space. In this he proved himself a worthy pupil of Labrouste and, above all, of Viollet-le-Duc.

SIR THOMAS DEANE AND BENJAMIN WOODWARD: INTERIOR OF THE UNIVERSITY MUSEUM AT OXFORD, ABOUT 1855.

HENRI LABROUSTE (1801-1875). THE READING-ROOM IN THE BIBLIOTHÈQUE NATIONALE, PARIS, 1855-1868.

ANATOLE DE BAUDOT (1834-1915). INTERIOR OF THE CHURCH OF SAINT-JEAN DE MONTMARTRE, PARIS, 1894-1904.

Obviously architecture has its own medium of expression which distinguishes it from the space of painting or that of sculpture; indeed, if there is any mingling of them architecture is bound to suffer, either by an excess of plastic or an excess of decorative effects. It is important to note, nevertheless, that at the very time when there arose a new painting which departed from traditional space-representation, there arose an architecture which also departed from traditional space-representation, employing materials whose lightness and flexibility created a new form and a new dimension. The Menier Chocolate Works, built by Jules Saulnier in 1871-1872, brought a decisive change in the relationships of masses which go to determine architectonic space, for the whole weight of the building is borne by an iron skeleton, the outer walls functioning simply as a curtain, not as weight-bearing members. In the same way Eiffel's Garabit Viaduct, with the structural lightness made possible by the flexibility of steel, went to define a space which, though logically different, brings to mind the contemporary pictorial constructions of the Impressionists.

In architecture too, then, we might say that there now occurred a transition from the shaded relief of the classical tradition to patterned volumes, from flat wall surfaces to a more open and varied design. Konrad Wachsmann has shown how this transition took place, tracing it from the predominance of straight, level surfaces in Paxton's Crystal Palace to the dissolution of masses which we find in the Firth of Forth Bridge near Edinburgh, built thirty years later by Fowler and Baker. But even in the work of Eiffel the arabesque of the metallic structure, whose visual appeal is enhanced in the Tower by the thickly patterned rivets on the girders, does not create plastic relief but volume in depth, with a complex internal perspective. The added dimension created by such recession, which arises out of the volumetric structure of the tower, is present again in the displacement of the piers of Dutert and Contamin's Galerie des Machines: they emphasized the dynamic direction of space and at the same time

EUGÈNE VIOLLET-LE-DUC (1814-1879). STUDY OF VAULTING.
FROM "ENTRETIENS SUR L'ARCHITECTURE," PARIS 1872.

JULES SAULNIER. THE MENIER CHOCOLATE WORKS
AT NOISIEL-SUR-MARNE, 1871-1872.

...TAVE EIFFEL (1832-1923).
...AIL OF THE EIFFEL TOWER,
...IS, 1887-1889.

...AVE EIFFEL (1832-1923).
...GARABIT VIADUCT OVER THE TRUYÈRE
...AL), 1880-1884.

...O

3

TECHNICAL DEVELOPMENTS

In 1867 John A. Roebling began work on the Brooklyn Bridge, for which he used steel cables over fifteen inches in diameter. Here, as one of the foremost building designers of our time, Konrad Wachsmann, has written, "technology had indirectly inspired a work, the effect of which is to demand the application of the concepts of art as a standard of value." We must bear this in mind in considering the great works of nineteenth-century engineering, and in examining the ideas and theories of the innovators. For Viollet-le-Duc art was a form of thought; it appeared wherever a rational order was imposed on structures. Viollet-le-Duc may not have been a great architect; but both by his writings and his actual handling of materials and techniques he contributed more than anyone to the renewal of architecture in the nineteenth century. As Pierre Francastel has observed, "He surpassed Cole and Laborde inasmuch as he saw the futility of a compromise between the arts and industry. It was he in fact who, in precise terms, voiced what was to be the great idea of the end of the century: that there exists a beauty directly bound up with the handling of techniques." Viollet-le-Duc saw the need for new structures, and consequently for new forms, at a time when the use of new materials made it absurd to imitate traditional forms and called, on the contrary, for the definition of a new spatial dimension.

defined it in relation to the machinery exhibited in the main hall and in relation to the *ponts roulants* (a kind of traveling crane) which carried spectators across the hall—this in accordance with a continually shifting, indeed a multiple perspective. Thus the piers did not mark a pause but were the key elements in the dynamic distribution of the different perspective vistas. While making all due allowance for the irreducible diversity of painting and architecture, the fact remains that there is a correspondence between Dutert and Contamin's dynamic conception of space and that of Cézanne, which led him about the same time to do away with traditional perspective in the rendering of space.

The use of metal thus led to momentous innovations in architectural design. For metal was more than a simple technical device; its use supplied the impetus for the creation of a type of architecture in keeping with the requirements and the artistic sensibility of the period. That impetus can even be seen in the work of tradition-bound or eclectic-minded architects like Alessandro Antonelli. The Mole Antonelliana, originally intended as the Israelite temple of Turin, rises to a height of 510 feet. No masterpiece, it is the fruit of a compromise between traditional structures reposing on columns and vaulted structures. Begun in 1863, it was carried through with difficulty and was only completed after the architect's death by his son Costanzo. It is, however, a work of some significance: while Antonelli had no opportunity of making any revolutionary use of metal, he succeeded in giving the brick dome all the lightness of a metallic construction. The vaulting, wrote Antonelli to the mayor of Turin in 1874, is "reduced to cellular form by means of the main vertical ribs joined together with arches comparable to metal spans." The Mole Antonelliana has been described as "a wonderful toy raised by a boy prodigy with a genius for mechanical science but ignorant of art." It is important, however, as an attempt to resolve two conflicting views of architecture and focus attention on technical developments.

ALESSANDRO ANTONELLI (1798-1888).
THE MOLE ANTONELLIANA AT TURIN.
BEGUN IN 1863.

FERDINAND DUTERT (1845-1906)
AND CONTAMIN (1840-1893).
DETAIL OF THE GALERIE DES MACHINES
AT THE PARIS WORLD'S FAIR OF 1889.
CONTEMPORARY PHOTOGRAPH BY CHEVOJON.

AMERICAN FUNCTIONALISM

After the Great Exhibition of 1851, Sir Henry Cole in England and Laborde in France showed unusual foresight in speculating on the future role of the young American nation, which even then was giving proof of its productive capacity and powers of organization. Both men saw its gathering strength and wondered how its intervention would affect a world and social order that could certainly no longer turn its back on the growing problems of industrial production and technological expansion. In coping with those problems Europe was handicapped by its cultural traditions, by its rootedness in the past, by political and social conditions very different from those of the United States, where such problems were viewed in quite another light. There the conflict between architect and engineer was far less radical, and the United States had opted decisively for industrialization. Above all, as Siegfried Giedion has shown, American industry proved capable of creating forms which, breaking more readily with styles and traditions of the past, were better adapted to the function they were meant to perform. Machinery and machine techniques were not expected to yield an equivalent of the handmade products of the past; they provided objects and implements whose design was conditioned by the process of manufacture and standardized in the interests of mass production. These methods were also applied to housing design and construction.

Students of American architecture have emphasized the importance of the so-called balloon frame —a type of timber framing with cross-beams placed at regular intervals to form a continuous support for floor, roof, and walls; this skeleton was then covered with clapboards. Light, well proportioned and sturdy, the balloon frame gave greater compactness and at the same time greater flexibility to the traditional American construction, and being a standardized element it simplified design and reduced costs. According to Giedion, who has identified George Washington Snow (1797-1870) as

the inventor of the balloon frame, this type of timber construction derives from methods already in use in the American colonies in the seventeenth century. Snow, a New Englander who moved out to Chicago in the 1830s, "started with these traditional methods, changing and adapting them to meet the new possibilities of production in a way which was as simple as it was ingenious" (Giedion).

As regards the use of metal frames, we have already referred to the work of James Bogardus, who was convinced that the new materials offered to the nineteenth-century architect could be adapted to any style. In the building he designed for the publishing house of Harper and Brothers in New York (1854), the façade, with its vast expanse of glass and its iron columns and arches, achieves a decorative effect very much in the Venetian style. His project—never executed—for the exhibition hall at the New York World's Fair of 1853 included a high central tower with a passenger elevator and iron girders supporting the roof. The building itself was designed as a circular amphitheater some twelve hundred feet in diameter, thus differing radically from the longitudinal plan of Paxton's Crystal Palace. Bogardus, moreover, made a point of keeping the cost of construction as low as possible.

Already before the middle of the century, then, technical improvements had been introduced which were bringing about a radical change in architectural design; there were, however, other factors at work in this process of change and renewal. The trends of American art in the nineteenth century were closely connected with those of European art, indeed they were almost completely dependent on them. This was also the case with architecture, anyhow up to the appearance of the Chicago School after 1880; and even the representatives of that school had studied in Europe. It is none the less true that international art forms are inevitably adapted to some extent to local requirements and traditions, and made to express the significant aspects of a particular condition or outlook. The first great school of American landscape painting, the Hudson River School, was an offshoot of European Romanticism, and nowhere is this truer than in the work of its finest exponents, Asher B. Durand and Thomas Cole, and in that of Thomas Doughty. But while their style differs little from that of the European Romantics, and Europe remained the source and background of their artistic culture, the American painters nevertheless looked at nature with fresh eyes, they discovered new horizons, saw a new grandeur in nature and approached it with the spirit of adventure that characterized the opening up of new territories in the North and West. This is evident even in the work of painters unconnected with the Hudson River School, like Albert Bierstadt, who followed the covered wagons westward in the 1850s, painting the Rocky Mountains and hunting scenes on the prairies. It is evident too in William Morris Hunt and George Inness, both Romantics who were influenced by the realism of the Barbizon School, and also in William Page and Thomas Eakins.

Romantic realism represents one of the best moments of nineteenth-century American painting, before the Impressionist mode came in towards the end of the century with artists like J. Alden Weir, Charles H. Davis, Ernest Lawson, Arthur Goodwin, Willard L. Metcalf, and above all Theodore Robinson, John H. Twachtman and Childe Hassam. The Realists were intent on conveying a direct vision of nature, of the unspoilt beauty and grandeur of American scenery. Something of the same spirit informed the writings of Fenimore Cooper first of all, then of the men who have come to be looked upon as representing a golden age of literature, the so-called American Renaissance: Emerson, Thoreau, Hawthorne, Melville, Whitman—writers who, whatever their affinities with contemporary European literature, have an indisputable originality. The young nation had begun to show strong features of its own, to express its forthright, highly individual character and build up a history which Europe could not afford to ignore. As Emerson put it, "things are in the saddle, and ride mankind."

The same breakthrough occurred in American architecture. Even in imitating European styles, as they did from the very beginning, American builders had to cope with various problems of adaptation, not so much in monumental buildings in towns as in domestic housing. Even the prevailing classical design on Hellenistic or Palladian lines was adjusted in the South to meet the needs of the plantation houses which were the characteristic type of construction along the Mississippi, in Louisiana, and in other southern states. From the time when the Thirteen Colonies won their independence and a new society began to take shape in the New World, American architects, whether born in Europe or America, were compelled to arrive at solutions for which there were no precedents, even though they were guided by the prevailing ideals of the period. Think of the new cities that were being laid out, of L'Enfant's plan of Washington (1790), Woodward's plan of Detroit (1807) and the plan of New York approved in 1811; the scale on which they were designed and the needs they were calculated to meet were unprecedented. Thus began that long line of development which, in a surprisingly short time, led to the original achievements of Richardson, the Chicago School, and Sullivan; and which, with the early work of Frank Lloyd Wright, laid the basis for one of the most distinctive types of architecture ever created by man.

All this was not only the outcome of technological advances. It sprang from a growing realization, in the minds of a free people, of their power to build and create; from the faith and optimism which colored their whole view of the world and society; above all from their determination to "make history" and weld themselves into a nation which took pride in its brief past and integrated it into the present, in a typically American sense of continuity. From the time of the Declaration of Independence and what has been called the Age of Jefferson, the United States consciously set about creating an architecture worthy of the new period of history in which the American people would be called upon to play an increasingly important part. The development of American art, of architecture in particular, cannot be considered apart from those democratic ideals which came to pervade the national consciousness. For Jefferson, who was not only the author of the Declaration of Independence and the first president to be inaugurated in Washington, but also designed the State House at Richmond (with Latrobe), his own mansion at Monticello and the original buildings of the University of Virginia, good architecture was an expression of the democratic consciousness. The same principle held good for Wright a century later, and Wright, like Sullivan before him, was known to be an admirer of America's great democratic bard, Walt Whitman.

The New England writers had a strong sense of architecture and its social implications, as also of its intimate connection with nature. Mention has already been made of Hawthorne's participation in Brook Farm, the experimental community founded by George Ripley in 1841 for "plain living and high thinking." With Emerson, who was a friend of Horatio Greenough's, appeared what we may call the "organic principle" of architecture inspired by the example of nature and its processes of organic growth. The French philosophers and sociologists had already put forward the naturalistic view; it was taken up by Ruskin and, as F.O. Matthiessen points out in his *American Renaissance*, it came to Emerson directly from Coleridge, who had written as follows: "The form is mechanic, when on any given material we impress a pre-determined form, not necessarily arising out of the properties of the material;—as when to a mass of wet clay we give whatever shape we wish it to retain when hardened. The organic form, on the other hand, is innate; it shapes, as it develops, itself from within, and the fullness of its development is one and the same with the perfection of its outward form. Such as the life is, such is the form. Nature, the prime genial artist, inexhaustible in diverse powers, is equally inexhaustible in forms..." These principles may lead to misunderstandings, may suggest a biological or merely naturalistic (i.e. imitative) interpretation of architecture. And indeed Emerson, as Matthiessen says, held that "beauty in art springs from man's response to forms in nature." But the organic principle will be correctly interpreted by those who are prepared to see in architecture an autonomous form of expression. Such was the case with Horatio Greenough, for whom organic structure and functionalism were one and the same thing.

Born in Boston in 1805, Greenough was a Neoclassical sculptor who studied under Thorwaldsen in Rome and lived for many years in Italy. A friend of Fenimore Cooper and Emerson, he himself wrote well both in prose and verse and took an active part in the cultural revival brought about by the New England writers. While little now remains of his work as a sculptor, he is entitled to rank alongside contemporary European innovators by virtue of his refusal to imitate past styles, his rejection of non-functional embellishment, and his identification of beauty with function, which led him to agree with Emerson that "the modern architecture is ship-building." Beauty, function, character, bound up inseparably in the design and realized in action —this, he held, must be the basis of architecture. "By beauty," he wrote, "I mean the promise of function, by action I mean the presence of function, by character I mean the record of function." Siegfried Giedion has rightly stressed the importance for American culture of these statements which consciously or unconsciously re-echo those of Labrouste in France. Greenough could write in 1843 that "the normal development of beauty is through action to completeness. The invariable development of embellishment and decoration is more embellishment and more decoration. The *reductio ad absurdum* is palpable enough at last; but where was the first downward step? I maintain that the first downward step was *the introduction of the first inorganic, non-functional element, whether of shape or color*." Beauty achieves completeness through action—in saying that Greenough anticipated by a hundred years the basic tenet of American abstract expressionism.

For Greenough, as for Ruskin and a little later for Morris, art can only thrive in a society based on equal rights for all. Imitation of the styles of the past was not only an aesthetic absurdity but an impediment thrown in the way of the progressive development of the individual. In pointing to ship-design as the highest expression of functional beauty, Greenough also had this to say: "Could we carry into our civil architecture the responsibilities that weigh upon our ship-building, we should ere long have edifices as superior to the Parthenon, for the purposes that we require, as the Constitution or the Pennsylvania is to the galley of the Argonauts." The imitation of forms which have lost the function for which they were designed, and excess of ornament, these were the cardinal sins that were estranging artistic expression from the spirit of the community. A building, after all, can hardly be designed exclusively in terms of its outward appearance. The architect must begin from the internal nucleus, from the heart of the building, and from this progress outwards, allowing all the while for its various functions. It is worth noting that as early as 1853 a

German architect, H. Riehl, was looking forward to the time when architectural design would no longer be expected to conform to the laws of mechanical symmetry and buildings would be designed from the inner core outwards, on organic lines similar to those on which social structures develop. The organic and functional principle which appears in Greenough's writings on architecture was therefore not based on mere literary assumptions, but rather on a shrewd appreciation of social realities, of American life as it really was; that principle did not ignore the machine but took account of actual conditions in an industrial society.

Greenough's ideas were unknown to the Chicago architects, and probably even to Henry Hobson Richardson, though he worked in New England after his return from Europe. They were however a sign of the times, a symptom of innovations that were on the way and came in full force in the work of Richardson himself, the first great independent-minded personality in American architecture. After graduating from Harvard in 1859, Richardson went directly to Paris and studied for a year at the Ecole des Beaux-Arts. When he returned to the United States and went into practice as an architect in New York, he at once set out on a path of his own, breaking away from eclecticism, classicism and English Gothic. Chary of ornamentation and aiming at extreme simplicity, he directed his attention not only to the structural properties of the materials employed but also to their aesthetic values, which in his hands became an organic part of the exterior of the building, serving to emphasize the relationships of masses in the definition of space. French Romanesque, with its sober lines and sincerity of expression, appealed so strongly to his sense for mass and broad simplification that he adopted that style in several buildings, as in the Brattle Square church in Boston (1870). But gradually he ceased to imitate, especially when he was allowed a certain freedom of design, as in Sever Hall at Harvard, which Bruno Zevi has described as "a genuine masterpiece because, working within a medievalizing system of volumes, he undulates his walls, breaks them up with large windows and triumphs with a masterly use of brick." His work culminated in his designs for the Marshall Field Wholesale Store in Chicago, whose construction was finished in 1887, a year after his premature death. This building had a decisive influence on the architects who were at work in Chicago and the Middle West. "Louis Sullivan himself," as Wright reminds us in *A Testament*, "kept an eye upon Richardson's superb use of stone in the arch."

Chicago was almost completely destroyed by fire in 1871. In the next ten years the city was in a ferment of reconstruction; this was also a time of intense cultural activity. In art circles the organic principles of the New England writers and the rationalist doctrines of Semper and Viollet-le-Duc were topics of lively discussion. The senior representative of what has been styled the Chicago School was William Le Baron Jenney. An engineer who had studied in Paris at the Ecole Polytechnique, he took part in the Civil War as a major in Sherman's corps of engineers and then taught at the University of Michigan. The Leiter warehouse in Chicago, which he designed in 1879, reveals already what were to be distinctive features of the new functional architecture. Everything is subordinated to the structure, to the ruthless exclusion of ornamental accessories and of any imitation of other styles that might falsify the functional design of the building. In the Home Insurance Building of 1885 Jenney exploited even more fully the possibilities of an iron skeleton in a skyscraper; in the Leiter Building of 1889 the metal skeleton in itself was sufficient to ensure the spatial definition of the edifice; the Manhattan Building of 1890 towered up to a height of sixteen storeys. From then on Jenney designed his buildings on a scale only possible in America, and in his studio the best architects in Chicago got their training: Daniel Burnham, Martin Roche and William Holabird. Burnham later went into partnership with John Root, who had been strongly influenced by Richardson. But the choice of Romanesque, as providing a basic working pattern, never limited the expressive possibilities open to these men, nor deflected them from the study of modern materials and techniques. It was Root who first used a trellis of iron rails bedded in cement to consolidate foundations sunk into marshy ground. Root and Burnham designed many notable buildings—the Western Union Building and the Turner House, in Chicago, and the Chronicle Building in San Francisco. The Monadnock Block in Chicago is also a remarkable piece of architecture, though it did not employ the skeleton construction but had walls of solid masonry. Of such modern office buildings Root himself wrote: "To lavish upon them profusion of delicate ornament is worse than useless... Rather should they by their mass and proportion convey in some large elemental sense an idea of the great, stable, conserving forces of modern civilization... Under these conditions we are compelled to work definitely with definite aims, permeating ourselves with the full spirit of the age, that we may give its architecture true art forms."

The most remarkable design produced by Roche and Holabird, working together, is that of the Tacoma Building of 1889; they also put up the Chicago Building of 1904, which is regarded as the last design executed in the spirit of the Chicago School. But the figure of Louis Sullivan stands out above all these technicians and architects. Born in Boston in 1856, Sullivan studied first at the Massachusetts Institute of Technology, then with Furness and Hewitt in Philadelphia. In 1873 he was in Chicago, working in the studio of William Le Baron Jenney. In 1874 he went to Paris and studied for a short time at the Ecole des Beaux-Arts. By 1875 he was back in Chicago. From 1881 to 1895 he was associated with an engineer, Dankmar Adler, and this was the most fruitful and significant phase of his career. He and Adler designed the Revell Building (1881), the Ryerson Building (1884), the Auditorium (1886-1890). In these years Sullivan achieved the full maturity of his expressive powers, as shown in the Getty family tomb (1890), the Exchange cold storage plant (1891), and above all the Wainwright Building in St Louis (1890-1891), perfect in its soaring verticalism, its fine proportions stemming directly from the functional structure, instead of being imposed by preconceived canons. For Sullivan regarded proportions as a result, not a cause. All this was made possible by his genius (there is no other word) as an architect, his ability to see beauty in terms of function, his keen sense of historical perspective and his instinctive grasp of the needs of his time and place. Architecture for him was a natural—not a naturalistic—process, and style the outcome of a perfect adaptation of the building to its setting. Science and technique he regarded as insufficient in themselves unless well seasoned with imagination. These ideas are brought home in his writings and sayings, and embodied in his work. His *Kindergarten Chats* contains a dialogue between himself and an imaginary pupil, to whom he says, referring back to Taine, that architecture is to be considered as a social science, that democracy must have a new expression in a democratic architecture, and that the outward form is the visible image of the spirit.

Sullivan's personality and ideas sum up a whole period of American culture, whose landmarks are those of his own career: the Chicago Stock Exchange (1893-1894); the Guaranty Building in Buffalo (1894-1895), one of the most beautiful skyscrapers ever built; the Gage Building (1898-1899); and the Carson, Pirie and Scott department store (1899-1904). The World's Columbian Exposition of 1893, which marked a relapse into classicism (whose forms even Burnham now accepted), dealt the death blow to the Chicago School. Of all the fair buildings, Sullivan's Transportation Building alone achieved a genuine coherence of design. As the only architect to accept no compromises, he found himself increasingly isolated. His work remains one of the outstanding architectural achievements of the nineteenth century, resolving as it did the conflict between art and technics. "Except for Louis Sullivan among the many poets I knew and have named," wrote Frank Lloyd Wright in *A Testament*, "there were then none among all the architects of this world. The poet had been too long absent from architecture. So long, indeed, architecture was no longer considered as a great creative art." Sullivan reasserted the validity, the integrity, of the creative urge that gives rise to great architecture. Wright began his work from these premises, but we may well ask ourselves to what extent Sullivan's moral example and his ideological position—not of course his style—has been reflected in recent years in the flowering of that typically American art form, action painting, which also lays so much stress on the creative urge.

the theories and practice of European architecture, to see the desirability and advantages of that unity, that "identical expression," and to work towards it single-mindedly. For building is not simply a matter of passively accepting the results of a new technique and opting, without any critical choice, for this or that structure. To build is, above all, to achieve a form of communication corresponding to the needs of the time, by means of certain materials and certain structures adapted to that purpose. The greatness of the Chicago architects lies in the fact that they met contemporary needs, without letting themselves be dazzled by the great styles of the past.

The Marshall Field Wholesale Store in Chicago, designed by Richardson, was the crowning achievement of his career. From a purely technical point of view there is nothing revolutionary about it; indeed the construction technique was traditional, and traditional too, in part, is its style and design. Yet this building had a momentous impact on the development of architecture in Chicago. The reason is that, for all its traditionalism, Richardson avoided the pitfalls of eclecticism, simplified and at the same time emphasized masses, and attained a satisfying rigor of design whose effect is enhanced by the organic unity into which the materials are welded. Richardson here exemplifies not a technique, for technical procedures lend themselves to many combinations, but an ideological commitment which henceforth became an indispensable part of the architect's aesthetic and working methods. This ideological element that went into the formulation of an architectural language enabled American builders to accept the products of contemporary technology without prejudice or suspicion.

Chicago in fact created an architecture that would have been inconceivable without the advances made in technology, not only as regards the actual manufacture of building parts (e.g. metal sections and the underpinning that replaced massive stone foundations) but as regards the accessories that permitted buildings to be designed on a certain scale. The skyscraper would have been useless without the invention of the elevator. (Similarly, one might say that open-air painting as practised by the Impressionists

HENRY HOBSON RICHARDSON (1838-1886). THE MARSHALL FIELD WHOLESALE STORE IN CHICAGO, 1885-1887. (CHICAGO ARCHITECTURAL PHOTO CO.)

WILLIAM LE BARON JENNEY (1832-1907). THE HOME INSURANCE BUILDING IN CHICAGO, 1883-1885.
(CHICAGO ARCHITECTURAL PHOTO CO.)

4

THE CHICAGO SCHOOL

The image most Europeans have of America is that of its skylines, the soaring profile of the great skyscrapers. These give cities like New York and Chicago a fascination and a beauty for which there is no counterpart in any other continent. The skyscraper has become the very symbol of modern America, of its empiricism and restless vitality. Over and above its architectonic value, which in many cases moreover is dubious, and in some non-existent, the skyscraper is the response to a need, the expression of a way of life. This type of building, exploiting all the resources of modern technology, came into being at the end of the nineteenth century, the brainchild of the group of architects known today as the Chicago School. As Siegfried Giedion has written, "The importance of the school for the history of architecture lies in this fact: for the first time in the nineteenth century the schism between construction and architecture, between engineer and architect, was healed. This schism marked the whole preceding part of the century. With surprising boldness, the Chicago school strove to break through to pure forms, forms which would unite construction and architecture in an identical expression."

The Americans were probably not the very first to resolve this conflict—we have seen what was being done in Europe—but they were certainly the first, thanks of course to all that they had learned from

DANIEL BURNHAM (1846-1912) AND JOHN ROOT (1850-1891). THE MONADNOCK BLOCK IN CHICAGO, 1889-1891.
(CHICAGO ARCHITECTURAL PHOTO CO.)

LOUIS SULLIVAN (1856-1924). THE CARSON, PIRIE AND SCOTT DEPARTMENT STORE IN CHICAGO, 1899-1904.
(CHICAGO ARCHITECTURAL PHOTO CO.)

was only rendered possible by the manufacture of paint-tubes.) When we remember the feverish activity, the economic expansion, the urge to progress and renewal that characterized Chicago in the years following the great fire of 1871, there is nothing surprising in so untraditional a conception of architecture. As Sullivan said, buildings went up ever higher because they expressed the drive, the pride, the exaltation, in a word the constructive fervor and love of innovation that pervaded not only architects but Chicagoans of all classes. So it was that the architectural style of Chicago at that time seemed unique, unparalleled by that of any other city or country. The Eiffel Tower, for example, not having the same structural function as the skyscraper, is conceived in an entirely different spirit.

Pure form, however, is not necessarily abstract: the horizontal widening of the windows, which created what has come to be known as the "Chicago window," is a feature that went to compensate the verticality of the edifice, which therefore is not a tower; at the same time the wider windows provided better lighting and a conveniently standardized element. The skeleton construction had the advantage, seen at once by William Le Baron Jenney, of lessening the danger of fire: Jenney's Home Insurance Building was the first to make use of an iron skeleton. Burnham and Root, on the contrary, kept in the Monadnock Block to outer walls of solid masonry and yet achieved an effect of absolute simplicity and straightforwardness by no means inferior to that obtained by Jenney. Even so, an architect like Louis Sullivan had no compunction about departing from verticalism and severely plain surfaces: despite its height, his Carson, Pirie, Scott and Company Department Store, of 1899-1904, is characterized by the horizontal organization of its façades, which extend along both sides of a corner site, at State and Madison streets, the "World's Busiest Corner." Here ornamentation reappears, based on naturalistic forms; freely but tastefully employed, it is well distributed and perfectly integrated into the structure. Sullivan thus resolved, more successfully than anyone else, the conflict between construction and architecture.

THE STRUCTURE OF VISION

Nearly all students of modern architecture agree that the renewal of architectural design was anticipated and influenced by the innovations of a number of painters working around 1890. According to Nikolaus Pevsner (to whom credit must go for reconstructing the cultural unity of this period), Cézanne, Gauguin and Van Gogh first of all, then Seurat, Denis, Munch, the Douanier Rousseau, Ensor, Toorop and Hodler, opposed their solid, substantial forms and forceful linework to the Impressionists' fleeting play of light and color; they opposed the expressive rendering of an inner vision to the Impressionists' adherence to a naturalistic way of seeing. This interpretation, however, takes it for granted—a view still widely held—that Impressionism was an extreme form of naturalism, that it was the ultimate expression of the credo of art for art's sake, and that it marked the end of one tradition rather than the beginning of another. Now, while it is true that about 1890 Cézanne, Gauguin, Seurat and Van Gogh introduced into painting an emotional dimension that had no precedent, it is equally true that all their researches are grounded on the premises laid down by the Impressionists; indeed those researches were sparked off by the crisis of Impressionism shortly after 1880. Not only Cézanne, who after 1877 ceased to exhibit with the Impressionists, but also Renoir, Sisley and above all Monet and Pissarro in the years after 1880 produced works which close analysis shows to be very different from those of the previous decade. Manet died in 1883, and Degas, though he had shared all the vicissitudes of the group and in fact had taken the most active part in organizing their exhibitions, had yet never wholly subscribed to the impressionist aesthetic. So that while no student of the period can deny the enormous importance of the renewal which took place about 1890, and which is at the origin of all subsequent developments of modern art, in painting as in sculpture and architecture, and even in music and literature, the fact remains that Impressionism marks the initial break with tradition.

We have already had occasion to note that the replanning of Paris was carried out by Baron Haussmann in the very years when the painting of Manet, Pissarro, Monet and Renoir, and also that of Jongkind, Boudin and Bazille, though it cannot yet be called impressionist, was nevertheless already committed to a definition of space which was departing more and more from the traditional conceptions of pictorial representation handed down from the Renaissance. Admittedly we cannot speak of Impressionism in the true sense until after 1870-1871 (and up to about 1880). Even so, it was during the 1860s that it took shape; it was then that artists gradually broke away from traditional modes of representation and left Romanticism and Realism behind. This was not only a period of technical discoveries and innovations when painters set up their easels in the open air and began juxtaposing—instead of blending—different shades and tones of color so as to render the shimmering play of sunlight; now, above all, painters repudiated academic traditions, opposed the prevailing taste and the institutions that upheld it, asserted the necessity for a new ideology, began looking at nature with fresh and inquiring eyes, and thus came to assign a different value to life and experience. The Salon des Refusés of 1863 was the first public exhibition of works testifying to this new outlook, and of these works Manet's *Déjeuner sur l'herbe* was the outstanding example. To react against academic painting and romantic sentimentalism, to render the play of light on the surface of objects and project that light on the picture plane and in depth as an effective form, not as an accidental accessory—this was the initial achievement which made a sharp breach with tradition, and which seemed all the more revolutionary because it expressed a different conception of the world.

The new outlook was based on the experience of reality—which is not to say that the natural world was regarded as an assemblage of immutable forms to be rendered with absolute fidelity. Pierre Francastel has aptly pointed out that the development of modern art which began with the Impressionists is characterized by a definitive rejection of panoramic vision, which gave way to a particular vision, and this choice in itself implies a rejection of realism or naturalism. To see what had happened, we need only observe the difference between a landscape by Daubigny and one by Monet. Neither the *Déjeuner sur l'herbe* nor *Olympia*, both painted by Manet in 1863, is an example of naturalism. The very word "impression"—which had been used before, notably by Corot—indicates the painter's fleeting contact with the phenomenon at the moment of inspiration; that contact supplied data which of course were not immutable but were on the contrary worked up and elaborated on. Pissarro's houses sometimes have no windows, not because they were really like that, but because the painter eliminated them in order to obtain a broader, light-reflecting surface. The great step taken by the Impressionists at the very start was their rejection of any transcendental metaphysic and their refusal to subordinate artistic procedures to those of nature. Everything was based on observation, but observation as it impinges on the conscious mind; it was the act of painting that created values, not the pure and simple transposition on to canvas of the results of observation. Here is where the Impressionists differed from the Realists and from Courbet himself.

After the *Déjeuner sur l'herbe* and *Olympia*, which as we have said were not yet impressionist paintings, Courbet's realism, which had been a point of departure even for Manet, could no longer serve as a guide; it no longer had any revolutionary elements to offer. All the more tenuous, then, was the link between the Impressionists-to-be and the Barbizon landscapists, including even Daubigny who was more sensitive than the others to the rendering of light. Even Zola, who had once urged artists to possess themselves of nature, could write in connection with Manet in 1866: "A work of art can only be the combination of a man, the variable element, and nature, the fixed element. The word 'realist' means nothing to me, holding as I do that reality must be subordinated to temperament." But the Impressionists went even further, for they saw in nature not a fixed element but only a momentary source of inspiration which the conscious mind seized on, transformed and reduced to a pictorial

motif. If it had transplanted the structures of the natural world on to canvas just as they present themselves to the eye, Impressionism would have produced nothing new; it would never have given us that new insight which a work of art must give; above all, it would never have exerted so decisive and enduring an influence. The structure of the impressionist vision was a linguistic structure and therefore autonomous; it created a unitary and coherent style, scaled to human requirements, as opposed to the "inhuman nature in which man makes his home" which Merleau-Ponty refers to in connection with Cézanne.

By virtue of the stylistic unity they achieved and the coherence of their pictorial vision, the Impressionists went beyond Realism and discredited it once and for all. When Renoir, Pissarro and Monet went out of doors and set up their easels on the banks of the Seine and Oise, they began—as Lionello Venturi has so clearly shown—to apply their paints in small separate touches suggesting the broken gleams of light on water. At first they painted water in this way but not the surrounding landscape; this they continued to represent in the accepted realist manner without emphasizing vibrations and luminosity. Such was their approach between 1867 and 1869. Then they perceived the resulting contrast, they saw how precarious was the coexistence of the two ways of seeing. They accordingly sacrificed the principle of naturalistic fidelity and attuned the landscape elements to the same vibration as the water: instead of quantitative, their procedure became qualitative. By the time the group came together again after the war of 1870 and the Commune, the new vision was mature and fully integrated. The hostility it aroused is understandable: it swept aside traditional taboos, it jolted a complacent public out of the groove of long-standing habits and conventions, it heralded the advent of a new generation alive to its responsibilities, it claimed its rightful place and function in a changing society. It was the very reverse of the monumental conceptions which Haussmann had tried to impose under the Second Empire, the very reverse of the sham history of the Gleyres and Coutures. It was a breath of life blowing away the literary sentimentalism of Ary Scheffer and his like.

The Impressionists admired and respected the masters to whom they owed so much—Corot, Delacroix and Courbet. But at the same time they felt that those masters, even though they maintained the highest standards, belonged ideologically to the past. We have noted that the spatial conception of Paxton's Crystal Palace, of Dutert and Contamin's Galerie des Machines, had no immediate antecedents because the function they were designed for, the needs they met, were new. The same is true of the Impressionists: their work does not answer to any previous outlook or condition of man. Modern painting accordingly begins with them, whereas the work of the English Pre-Raphaelites, though they had a deeper sense of the moral responsibility implicit in artistic creation, remains a mere episode linked to the past rather than to the future. This is not to say that impressionist painting is devoid of social implications—on the contrary. The late Lionello Venturi, who brought an unrivaled discernment and scholarship to the study of Impressionism, pointed out that the hostility of the public was due to various factors. "The Commune had frightened people to the point of making them blind and unfair. The prosecution of Courbet is a case in point. The political repercussions lasted for years: it was not until 1879 that MacMahon was forced to resign the presidency of the Republic. In the painting of the school of 1830, and even more in that of the Impressionists, there was a social undercurrent that ran deep. If the public called so obstinately for a clear and acceptable *subject*, if even Duret thought the elm trees of his friend Pissarro to be *vulgar*, it was because of a very widespread social prejudice. The Impressionists were men of the people, or of a lower middle class very close to the people. Those who cared for painting were men of the nobility or the upper middle class, and their taste had on the whole been respected by painters hitherto, with the exception of Daumier, whom they ignored. They sensed a social danger in the painting of the Impressionists. The charm of Renoir was no longer that of the boulevard but of the suburb, Pissarro's peasant women were still more rustic than Millet's, Monet's revolutionary power burst from his locomotives like a whiff of smoke, and Cézanne's outlook, like Zola's, was that of an anarchist."

The Impressionists refused to abide by the old principle that the subject of a picture must be lofty, beautiful, edifying. They did indeed choose particular elements of nature and of objects—but any objects, any aspect of nature. In their hands moreover the pictorial structure was not static but dynamic. Their vision was not analytic but synthetic; where naturalism would have called for an analysis of phenomena the Impressionists performed a synthesis. Of Manet Zola wrote: "His whole nature inclined him to see in terms of patches, of simple and energetic fragments. Of him it may be said that he was content to seek out accurate tones and juxtapose them on canvas. The result was that the canvas was covered with a sound and vigorous piece of painting. In the picture I find a man eager to get at the truth, and to draw from the truth a world that lives a peculiar and powerful life of its own." Notwithstanding the naturalistic premises, Zola here recognized the autonomy of Manet's pictorial idiom. Ten years later another critic, Emile Blémont, wrote as follows. "What is an impressionist painter? We have not been given any very satisfactory definition, but it appears to us that the artists who group themselves, or are grouped by others, under that designation are pursuing in various ways a similar purpose: to record with absolute sincerity the impression aroused in them by aspects of reality, using broad and simple means, contriving and attenuating nothing..." The Impressionists, he continued, "are synthesists, not analysts, and in this we believe them to be right; for if analysis is the scientific method *par excellence*, synthesis is the true procedure in art. They abide by no other law but the necessary relationships of things with each other; like Diderot, they think that the idea of the beautiful is the perception of these relationships."

In this sense Manet's *Olympia* already marks an advance on his *Déjeuner sur l'herbe*, painted in the same year, and the progress is not only a matter of bolder and more elaborate pictorial effects. In the *Déjeuner* Manet had not yet by any means freed himself from preoccupations of a naturalistic order, and space, though rendered vibrant by a subtle atmospheric coloring, obeys the traditional laws of perspective. In *Olympia* those laws begin to be violated, and the cubic space of tradition gives place to a different sequence of pictorial moments, in accordance with proportional norms never subsequently recognized. The *Déjeuner* is still bound up with documentary representation, so much so that, as is well known, the figure group was taken from a sixteenth-century engraving by Marcantonio Raimondi. *Olympia*, while it may bring to mind the Venuses of Giorgione or Titian, is emphatically not a historical document. Manet took a subject, which he arranged to suit himself, and made it contemporary by the addition of various "heretical" accessories (the cat, the flowers, the shoes worn by the nude woman, the Negress). The beauty of the picture springs from the relationships referred to by Blémont; it does not lie in the actual representation of a reality, even less is it a matter of symmetry or proportions; it is in a word the outcome of an experimental elaboration of the data of perception. From now on, the very conception of the function, purpose and utility of the painter's art was changing, slowly but radically. As we know from Antonin Proust, Manet considered it insulting to an artist to be described as a history painter; hence his revolt against the old "hierarchy of genres" and the notion that certain subjects were intrinsically nobler than others.

The subject thus came to assume less importance in the eyes not only of Manet but of all the Impressionists—this as a result of the altered conditions of society, of the democratic trend which a French writer, as noted earlier, described as the *fin des notables*. The diminishing importance of the subject was a key factor in the development of a new artistic sensibility, a sensibility which we still share today, a century later. Since the subject is necessary only in so far as it provides an initial stimulus, it does not matter, in the artistic process which absorbs it, whether it is ennobled, defined, superimposed hierarchically on the picture space, made imposing by well-balanced design, or equated with a canon of ideal beauty. The Impressionists were the first painters of the modern age to deal a serious blow at the idol of beauty, or better, the first to arrive at another type of beauty through a handling of color which in itself contradicted the traditional conception of form bound by closed contours. The emphasis they laid on color values, and above all on light values, was in the first place a critical choice; in a sense it might be said to correspond to the adoption of metal structures by architects. For just as the metal structure necessarily modified the forms and modules of building design, so the emphasis on color modified the conception of form, the perspective and space, the visual norms of the picture. Just as metal structures tended to lighten the masses, so the use of luminous colors—and light itself is the real subject of impressionist pictures—led to the break-up of traditional schemes of representation. The intensification of color and light therefore takes on a revolutionary significance, not only on the technical plane but above all on that of behavior. "To read what was said of color by Ingres, Gleyre, Gérome and the other great teachers of the nineteenth century," writes Sir Kenneth Clark in *Landscape into Art*, "one would suppose that it was some particularly dangerous and disreputable form of vice. This was a rearguard action of idealist philosophy which had maintained that form was a function of the intellect, color of the senses. The belief was philosophically unsound, and had proved a real obstacle to free and sincere expression for centuries. Its removal gained a new liberty for the human spirit."

The parity—as against the old subordination of the artist—which Impressionism at last established between the artist and reality, had been led up to of course by the work of the vanguard painters immediately preceding the Impressionists. It was, nevertheless, largely the result of a new approach to painting. The Realists, and even the Romantics, had for the most part merely substituted one subject for another, choosing themes more closely connected with the realities of contemporary life in preference to the historical scenes and idealized figures of Neoclassicism; but the subject, though closer to real life, retained all its representational importance. The Impressionists, on the other hand, applied one and the same principle—that of "treating the subject for its tones and not for the subject itself," as Georges Rivière put it in 1877—to everything which met their eye and from which they drew inspiration. Courbet's landscapes, and even his luminous, highly simplified seascapes, are still given a monumental presentation. In him, a social commitment had been substituted for academic vacuity, and that commitment had been so intensely felt as to modify the traditional style, carrying it beyond Classicism and Romanticism. Courbet's development, as regards his simplification of images and concrete presentment, has analogies on the theoretical plane with that of Henry Hobson Richardson, but his treatment of space, like Richardson's, is still of the Renaissance type and the pictorial form is closed and delimited. Space and figure, that is, may be interdependent, but each is defined on the basis of different characteristics. The Impressionists did away with this distinction; the result was to give a new value to space which itself became an image and, by the same token, a psychological and emotional presence.

All this was the fruit of a new attitude towards natural phenomena. Deeply rooted in reality, drawing its vitality from nature, impressionist painting actually took from nature however only a few elements, just enough for the artist to keep his feet on the ground. For the Impressionists repudiated anything in the way of mythology, such as had enabled academic painters to idealize history and others to idealize nature. They were not pantheists. Their attitude to reality was open-minded and unprejudiced. With them sensibility, far from overshadowing reason, went hand in hand with it in order to produce that normative procedure which is necessary for the creation of autonomous expressive values. With the Impressionists for the first time, painting, and landscape painting in particular, was freed from that sense of mystery, those mythological and mystical overtones, and that documentary preoccupation, which had almost always characterized it in the past. A landscape was no longer a view. The figure painting ceased to be a state portrait or a glorification of the beauty of the human body. The still life ceased to be an ostentatious display of accumulated objects. The manner of representation changed because artists realized they were living in a changing world, not in a society whose structures were thought to be fixed once and for all. Their expressive values were those of men who regarded art as embracing the whole reality of the human condition, as pre-supposing a wholehearted participation in life as it is, over and above the mere concern with representation. Realism and naturalism became antithetical terms. For the Impressionists reality did indeed mean the acceptance of the data of perception, but above all it meant the further elaboration of those data in the crucible of one's own experience and behavior.

WINSLOW HOMER (1836-1910). CROQUET SCENE, 1866. ALBRIGHT-KNOX ART GALLERY, BUFFALO, N.Y.

GIOVANNI FATTORI (1825-1908). SENTINELS: THE WHITE WALL, ABOUT 1886. COLLECTION OF COUNT GAETANO MARZOTTO, VALDAGNO.

WINSLOW HOMER AND FATTORI

Winslow Homer is one of the outstanding American painters of the nineteenth century. Born and brought up in Boston, he studied for a few years in New York but belonged by temperament and taste to that New England culture which was so instrumental in shaping a characteristically American sensibility. In 1866 he went to France, but even before that he had broken with the academic tradition and turned back to nature, following on his own a path parallel to that of the French artists of his time. The picture reproduced here dates from just before his trip to Europe. It is a simple, straightforward open-air scene, almost a genre scene, but rendered with rapid strokes of the brush, and flooded with a light so strong as to bleach the colors. It is not an impressionist painting; the vision and the breaking up of the touch are not unitary or synthetic and betray a concern with descriptive analysis. This Croquet Scene *shows nevertheless that even outside Europe, and only a few years after the middle of the century, there was a painter sensitive enough to light to bathe the whole picture in it and subordinate all else to a bold analysis of light effects. "I have never tried to do anything," wrote Homer, "but get the proper relationship of values." Those words might have been uttered by a French Impressionist.*

Giovanni Fattori was the greatest Italian painter of the nineteenth century and the leading personality of the "Macchiaioli" group, the only forward-looking movement in Italian painting of this period. The name derives from the word macchia, *meaning a "patch" or "blob" of color. Experiments with the color patch were being made in Italy as early as 1858, but it was only after the war of independence of 1861 that these Tuscan artists joined forces and began exploring in earnest the possibilities of constructing the entire picture, both figures and setting, with small touches of color. What they too aimed at was a compositional synthesis, but while in many ways they were very close to the Impressionists, the work of the Macchiaioli suffers in comparison from their limited capacity to transform the data of perception and spatial representation. Even so, their use of the color patch brought Italian painting into the current of contemporary art, lifting it from the slough of the past and turning it decisively towards the future. Many of Fattori's most successful pictures represent soldiers, and the* White Wall *is one of the finest, evoking so well an atmosphere of anxious expectation, all action momentarily suspended in the sultry stillness of a noonday sun so bright that even shadows are interwoven with light.*

"The impressionist eye," wrote Jules Laforgue, "is the most advanced eye in the evolution of mankind." And indeed the optical sensitivity of the Impressionists had no precedent. For this very reason Impressionism was not a mere formula which any painter could take over and apply for purposes of his own. Cézanne, coming to Impressionism about 1872, brought to it a particularly strong sense of pictorial construction, as shown by the House of Père Lacroix of 1873—a sense, instinctive with him, of which there is little sign in Renoir's flower piece of 1876. But it is difficult to draw any parallel between Renoir and his friends, for one of his main contributions to the development of the impressionist way of seeing lay in his determination never to cleave to any hard-and-fast program; for him the painting of every picture, whether still life, figure piece or landscape, was a fresh experience. Pissarro was more akin to Cézanne, and each had a salutary influence on the other. The landscapes Pissarro executed between 1872 and 1877 represent in fact a constructive synthesis; their powerful, forthright effects of spatial recession make them, however, quite different from the landscapes Cézanne painted with so decisive a mastery of formal design.

Manet, with his masterpieces of 1863, had paved the way for the new painting. Ten years later, won over completely to the impressionist vision, he found in it the answer to all his problems and freed himself from the thrall of the subject. The Rue de Berne with Bunting, painted only five years before his death, is one of his finest works; it reveals Manet's wonderful ability to record what he saw and felt in painterly terms incomparably rich and pure. In all the Impressionists, even Manet, we can feel the vivifying effects of Monet's influence; his visual sensitivity and his way of rendering forms by means of light vibrations alone, even to the extent of refashioning traditional space and volumes, contributed very largely to the renewal of painting both in his lifetime and thirty years after his death. In Monet more than any other painter, the integration of form, light and matter is such that the motif loses its contingent character.

Something of that perfection is occasionally achieved by Sisley too, whose best work belongs to the impressionist period, when the very spirit of poetry breathes through his pictures, which sparkle with delicately tinted gleams of light, as in his snowscapes, where muted touches of pink and blue flicker and vibrate in a continuous movement that transforms the ostensible motif into pure painting.

PAUL CÉZANNE (1839-1906). THE HOUSE OF PÈRE LACROIX AT AUVERS, 1873.
NATIONAL GALLERY OF ART, WASHINGTON, D.C. CHESTER DALE COLLECTION.

AUGUSTE RENOIR (1841-1919). BOUQUET IN FRONT OF A MIRROR, 1876. PRIVATE COLLECTION.

CAMILLE PISSARRO (1830-1903). WOODLAND PATH, SUMMERTIME, 1877. LOUVRE, PARIS.

EDOUARD MANET (1832-1883). RUE DE BERNE WITH BUNTING, 1878. BÜHRLE COLLECTION, ZURICH.

CLAUDE MONET (1840-1926). RUE MONTORGUEIL WITH BUNTING, 1878. MUSÉE DES BEAUX-ARTS, ROUEN.

AUGUSTE RENOIR (1841-1919). PATH IN THE WOODS, 1874. PRIVATE COLLECTION.

ALFRED SISLEY (1839-1899). SNOW AT LOUVECIENNES, 1878. LOUVRE, PARIS.

CLAUDE MONET (1840-1926). SUNFLOWERS, 1881. THE METROPOLITAN MUSEUM OF ART, NEW YORK.
BEQUEST OF MRS H.O. HAVEMEYER, 1929, THE H.O. HAVEMEYER COLLECTION.

Much of the nineteenth century is barren of high-quality sculpture. It is not difficult to see why this was so: the public, or rather the authorities who were the sculptors' chief patrons, were only interested in pompous, ostentatious works of a commemorative order, and sculpture, more than painting, is subject to the desires of patrons. When sculptors met those desires and satisfied them, they automatically cut themselves off from the main line of artistic development which was evolving in quite another direction—away from the glorification of heroes. It was the painters who showed the way. Even before Rodin and Medardo Rosso, who were at work in the later decades of the century, the great sculptors of the nineteenth century were Daumier and, after him, Degas and Gauguin; Bonnard too, it is well to remember, was active as a sculptor. So it was in large measure due to the efforts of painters that the art of sculpture regained the high standing it had lost.

If we look at a painting by Degas, we realize that, in accordance with the principles of the impressionist vision to which the artist subscribed (though not completely by any means), the picture achieves a synthesis of figure and setting by "enhancing the plastic, autonomous and concrete qualities of space" (Pierre Francastel). In his sculpture Degas aims at the same enhancement: the surrounding space is not amorphous but is suggested and indeed defined by the movement of the figure. Degas moreover modeled his figures in wax, a medium which makes possible particular accentuations and plays of light. Optical sensitivity becomes plastic sensitivity, and the modeling, instead of being merely a uniform envelope, acquires color values.

Rodin and Medardo Rosso were the sculptors who most closely approximated to the researches of the Impressionists, Rodin with his symbolic preoccupations, Medardo Rosso by starting out from a naturalism which was soon redeemed by the luminous transformation of figures. Both men restored to sculpture a vibrancy which the smooth modeling of tradition had completely sacrificed. In the Head of the Crouching Woman *Rodin hollowed out the face to create a more dynamic play of light. Medardo Rosso on the contrary attenuated the facial volumes in his* Evening Impression on the Boulevard *in order to gain a broader light-reflecting surface. The result in both cases is a piece of sculpture which conveys the underlying implications of contemporary history.*

EDGAR DEGAS (1834-1917). END OF AN ARABESQUE, 1877. LOUVRE, PARIS.

EDGAR DEGAS (1834-1917). GRANDE ARABESQUE, THIRD TIME (SECOND STUDY), 1882-1891. WAX. LOUVRE, PARIS.

AUGUSTE RODIN (1840-1917). HEAD OF THE CROUCHING WOMAN (STUDY FOR "LA LUXURE"), 1882. BRONZE.
COLLECTION OF MRS EMIL L. FROELICHER, NEW YORK.

MEDARDO ROSSO (1858-1928). EVENING IMPRESSION ON THE BOULEVARD, 1893. WAX.
GALLERIA NAZIONALE D'ARTE MODERNA, ROME.

ORDERED SENSATIONS

Cézanne was the first to see the necessity of going beyond Impressionism. He began to draw away from it in 1877, and the years from 1877 to 1882 were for him a period of intense research and meditation. What he was aiming at was a constructive synthesis of flat pattern and solid form. He only achieved this later, but even now he concentrated all his energies on this effort, working alone in jealous isolation and producing still lifes, landscapes, portraits and bathers with bold and majestic volumes. He was continually moving to and fro between the Ile-de-France and his native Provence. He remained on friendly terms with the Impressionists, and when Renoir paid him a visit at L'Estaque in February 1882 and fell ill, Cézanne looked after him devotedly. But he felt himself to be a lone wolf, took no further part in the group exhibitions, and occasionally passed judgment rather harshly on his old companions, whom he nevertheless respected and appreciated both as men and artists. "Monet is only an eye, but what an eye!" he once exclaimed, and the admiring homage of the last phrase does not abate the reservations implied in the first. In a letter to Joachim Gasquet he wrote that "in the painter are two things, the eye and the brain, and both must help each other out by turns; we must therefore work towards their mutual development, but as painters; we must exert ourselves to develop the eye for its vision of nature, and to develop the brain for the logic of ordered sensations which give us our means of expression." This is not to be construed as a general theory of painting; it was a simple observation, fruit of Cézanne's own experience. Yet it stands as a principle which, as exemplified in his pictures, has actually shaped the whole subsequent evolution of art. The painter laid down the validity of his own working methods, of the process whereby he organized what he saw. Reason and sensation coincide, and *la petite sensation*, as Cézanne called it, found in the rationality of that process the logical structures of its expression.

This attitude towards painting, which amounted to a revaluation of technique as a human activity, and therefore as a moment of history, was not however an intellectual attitude and had no scientific pretensions. The impressionist painters, and Cézanne with them, were not theorists; all their ideas were grounded on actual practice as painters and they never had any intention of devising a general theory of aesthetics. His son Lucien having raised the question of aesthetics, Pissarro wrote to him as follows. "Aestheticism is a kind of romanticism more or less blended with mere pretense, it is a way of tracing out for oneself a crooked path. There were some who tried to make of Impressionism a theory of this kind, while in reality Impressionism could not be other than a theory of pure observation, with no loss of fantasy, freedom, greatness and all that in the end makes an art great." But the painters of the younger generation were intent on giving a solid theoretical and scientific basis to the intuitions of Impressionism. The eighth and last group exhibition of the Impressionists, held in Paris in 1886, included works by Seurat and Signac, among them Seurat's most famous painting, *A Sunday Afternoon on the Island of La Grande Jatte*. Monet, Renoir, Sisley and Caillebotte, however, refused to take part, objecting to the presence of Seurat and Signac, as did Eugène Manet, brother of the artist (who had died in 1883). A conflict had now broken out between those who were designated as pure or romantic Impressionists and a younger group who styled themselves Neo-Impressionists or scientific Impressionists, that is to say Divisionists.

"For the first time," wrote Signac, "there now appeared works painted solely with pure, separated, balanced tones, which blend optically according to a logical method." Thus, for the Impressionists' intuitive handling of color, it was hoped to substitute a scientific procedure, but without sacrificing the conquest of light and the anti-naturalistic treatment of space; these indeed the Neo-Impressionists exploited to the full, taking them as primary data of vision. Where, in the opinion of the new painters, Impressionism had been spontaneous and impulsive, Divisionism was to be reflective and methodical. While fully recognizing the merits of the Impressionists, in particular that of having banished from their palette all but pure colors, Signac reproached them for not going far enough, for not having worked out a method. The distinction had become a technical one; the substantial difference between Signac and Seurat on the one hand and the Impressionists on the other lay in the fact that the former trusted to science and gave a symbolic value to the main lines of the composition. For them too, though in a different manner from that of Cézanne, the sensation had to be filtered through the mind which alone could organize it into logical structures. The composition was functional in that it did not conceal the method of elaboration, but left it clearly indicated together with the dynamic rhythms; the method coincided with the expressive value. "Some writers and critics," said Seurat, "see poetry in what I have done. No, I apply my method and that's all there is to it." A picture by Seurat, then, does not simply belong to a later phase of Impressionism; the substitution of method and thought for intuition reveals a different attitude of the individual towards the culture and society of the time. The creative act proceeded along deliberately scientific lines; art went hand in hand with science and took over its experimental methods in so far as they serve as instruments of knowledge.

The Impressionists had come intuitively to use small separate touches of pigment in order to convey the shimmer of light; they were never addicted to the study of scientific writings. The Neo-Impressionists, Seurat, Signac, Angrand, Luce, Cross, Dubois-Pillet and all their followers were acquainted with the theories of N. O. Rood, David Sutter, Maxwell, Helmholtz and above all with Chevreul's book *De la loi du contraste simultané des couleurs et de l'assortiment des objets colorés*, which had been published in 1839 and was reissued in 1889. A professor of chemistry who for some years was in charge of the laboratory of the Gobelins tapestry works, Chevreul had some acquaintance with the problems of painting and his definition of the simultaneous contrast of colors undoubtedly exerted a great influence on the Neo-Impressionists. "Looking at once at two unequally intense zones of a single color," wrote Chevreul, "and at two equally intense zones of different colors juxtaposed to them, that is contiguous to them on one side, the eye will perceive, if the zones are not too wide, some modifications which in the first case concern the intensity of the color, and in the second the optical composition of the two colors respectively juxtaposed. Since these modifications make the two zones, seen at the same time, appear more different than they really are, I designate them as a *simultaneous contrast of colors* and I call *contrast of tone* the modification based on the intensity of color, and *contrast of color* the modification based on the optical composition of each juxtaposed color." The simultaneous contrast of colors, as rationally tested and demonstrated by science, was to be the technical basis of the new painting. According to Signac, the Neo-Impressionists used only pure colors (as in fact the Impressionists had done before them), but they also rejected "any mixing on the palette, except the mixing of colors that stand next to each other in the color scale"; they took care moreover not to tarnish that purity with extraneous elements. Each pigment taken pure from the palette will be equally pure on the canvas; the optical mixture will take place there, once the colors have been laid in, in small separate touches, and their contrast will yield the maximum luminosity and, at the same time, a balance between tones and luminosity, always in accordance with the law of optical contrast, of the gradation of color and its irradiation. This procedure conferred on the work its flawless harmony.

For Seurat, in fact, art *is* harmony. He summed up his ideas in a letter written in 1890 to his friend the writer Maurice Beaubourg. "Harmony implies an analogy of the contraries, and also of the similarities, of tone, hue and line, considered according to their dominants and under the influence of light, in gay, calm or sad combinations." To this he added a few comments from the aesthetic and technical viewpoints. "Given the phenomena of the duration of a light-impression on the retina, a synthesis necessarily ensues. The means of expression is the optical mixture of the tones and hues (local color and color resulting from illumination: sun, oil lamp, gas and so on), that is to say of lights and their reactions (shadows), in accordance with the laws of contrast, gradation and irradiation. The compositional organization is in the harmony opposed to that of the tones, hues and lines of the picture."

In reality the aesthetic and technical viewpoints coincide; the aesthetic problem, and not for Seurat alone, became a problem of the organization, structure and architecture of that light-sensation which Impressionism had conquered. For Seurat painting meant "hollowing out the canvas"—that is, giving it depth, organizing it in space. His way of seeing was the very antithesis of Monet's, for with Monet the structure of the images tended to display itself on the surface; it was also very different from that of Cézanne, who ignored symbolic implications.

Seurat was already aiming at a new fusion of impressionist tones in the pictures he exhibited in 1884, like the *Bathers at Asnières* and the studies for the *Grande Jatte*. What he learned from Impressionism had enabled him to throw off the restraints of his academic training and go beyond the Barbizon brand of realism. But he had not yet carried divisionism to the limit nor explored all the possibilities of the simultaneous contrast of colors. His *Bathers at Asnières*, therefore, did not fully correspond to the pictorial organization he aspired to. The *Grande Jatte* on the other hand, painted between 1884 and 1886, has a well-knit architecture which systematically organizes all the light-perceptions. Its space is not uniform but multiple, echeloned in depth on various planes which are held together by the molecular sequence of color dots; his divisionism then, his use of minute, separate touches of pigment, was intended not only to step up the intensity of light but also to effect a synthesis of spatial elements. The images are built up into a rigorous structure, a geometric pattern which creates those dynamic directional lines which the Futurists, who were much indebted to Divisionism, were to call "lines of force." The methodical approach, however, was never carried to the point of abstraction. Seurat's method in fact is seen at its clearest in those pictures where he perceived the emotive potential of the light-impression, as in the landscapes painted between 1886 and 1891, the year of his death. Even so, he was never a passive spectator of nature, but always sought to interpret it, to record a reality transcending circumstances of time and place, of mood and fancy (much as Mondrian did later). He analyzed its structures as perceived by the eye, in this following in the steps of the Impressionists, and reconstructed them on canvas, recast them into an autonomous synthesis. The process by which he arrived at this synthesis was a conscious, deliberate one.

These preoccupations were shared by Signac, who was even more active than Seurat as a theorist of Divisionism. For him Neo-Impressionism was based on four fundamental principles: the impressionist palette, the optical mixture, the divided brushstroke, and a methodical, scientific technique. The Impressionists, as Signac saw it, had rendered light with far greater intensity than anyone before them (Delacroix, for example), but they had dimmed the splendor of their colors by failing to observe more strictly the laws that govern their harmony. The Neo-Impressionists on the other hand, by keeping exclusively to the optical mixture of pure colors, banishing every impurity from their pigments, methodically applying them in divided touches and observing the scientific theory of color, achieved the maximum in the way of luminosity, color intensity and harmony, beyond any previous painters. Such were Signac's claims. And while in fact his own pictures do appear more luminous than the Impressionists' and even Seurat's, the optical effects are so carefully calculated that the light seems more objective and somewhat lacking in warmth. Space moreover is too demonstratively rendered in terms of three dimensions.

In 1887 Seurat exhibited the *Grande Jatte* at the Salon des Vingt in Brussels; and there two years later, reinvited by the same group, he exhibited his *Poseuses* or *Models*. At that time Brussels was an active cultural center, in some ways more receptive than Paris to innovations not only in painting but in literature and music. The group of twenty painters known as Les Vingt held regular exhibitions; in 1886 they invited Odilon Redon to take part, in 1888 Signac and Toulouse-Lautrec, in 1889 Seurat and Gauguin, in 1890 Signac and Cézanne; and in 1891 they held a Van Gogh retrospective. The Belgian painters A. W. Finch and Theo van Rysselberghe were among the first to espouse Divisionism, and on Henry van de Velde the *Models* exerted an even greater influence than the *Grande Jatte* because of its "mobile and undulating lines." Seurat's painting, together with that of Gauguin, Van Gogh and the Symbolists, was a fundamental component of Art Nouveau, whose first valid works were produced in Belgium by Horta and Van de Velde. Spreading not only to Belgium but all over Europe, Divisionism went far to revitalize the old pictorial culture, though it owed its impact more to its visual appeal and luminosity than to its structural values.

Indeed, European Divisionism nearly always emphasized symbolic elements to the detriment of compositional rigor; it interpreted reality on literary and "decadent" lines. But the lesson of Seurat proved to be of fundamental importance for several of the great movements of early twentieth-century painting, Fauvism and Futurism.

Of the original Impressionists, only Pissarro, together with his son Lucien, embraced Divisionism. We can see why he did so when we remember that even in his most characteristically impressionist paintings of the 1870s he had shown a constant concern for sound design and construction, and in this respect greatly influenced Cézanne. By means of divisionist methods Pissarro hoped to realize that ideal of solid structure which he always held before him. He subscribed wholeheartedly to Seurat's ideas, and in a letter to Durand-Ruel written in 1886 he modestly admitted that he had done no more than "follow, with my colleagues Signac and Dubois-Pillet, the example set by Seurat." Like him, Pissarro proposed to "attempt the modern synthesis" on the strength of the theories of Chevreul, Rood and Maxwell, to "substitute the optical mixture for the mixing of pigments on the palette"—in other words to break down tones "into their constituent elements, seeing that the optical mixture produces a far more intense luminosity than blended pigments." He recognized, however, that the system could not be valid for everybody, "since the sole originality consists in the character of the drawing and the particular vision of each artist."

The scientific side of Divisionism could not but appeal to Pissarro. He was a socialist and believed in progress as contributing to the improvement of social conditions. Science, he felt, would help to relieve human life of its toil and drudgery; with its logical procedures it would impose new social structures of an equally logical nature and therefore more just. The human aspirations implicit in Pissarro's scientific idealism are reflected in his painting now, just as they had been in his impressionist days. Félix Fénéon said of him that he brought "to Neo-Impressionism his mathematical rigor of analysis and the authority of his name"; Lionello Venturi noted that what he contributed above all was his spontaneous and impulsive faith. Pissarro's divisionist pictures have none of the hieratic stylization of Seurat's. Marking a clear distinction between foreground and background, he built up a three-dimensional composition with rapid touches of color; but the light intensity is the product of an imaginative intuition and space is therefore not reduced to a geometric pattern. Pissarro accepted the theory and technique of Divisionism, but what he was after even more than simultaneous contrasts was the blending of tones. His enthusiasm however lasted only a few years; by 1890 he was already moving away from Divisionism.

While Seurat, Signac and Pissarro were demonstrating the efficacity of their methods and affirming the principle of "ordered sensations" as a means of going beyond the impressionist way of seeing, all the artists who had created Impressionism were engaged in working out fresh solutions. Renoir confessed at one point that he had come to "a dead-end." When in 1881 he went to Italy and discovered what he called the "wisdom of Raphael," the admiration he felt for that wisdom, which he saw through the intermediary of Ingres, had the effect of cramping his own style for a time. But his spirits were too exuberant to be kept long in check, and by 1885 he was again giving them free rein. Even Monet, the Impressionist *par excellence*, took to the methodical analysis of light values. Commenting in 1880 on the evolution of Impressionism, he admitted that what had been a church had become a commonplace school open to all comers. The imitators, like Fantin-Latour and Bastien-Lepage, were overlaying Impressionism with a sentimental veneer, misrepresenting it completely. Impressionism had built, nevertheless, the indispensable foundation on which all forward-looking artists took their stand, even the new men who were proposing more dramatic solutions—Gauguin, Toulouse-Lautrec, Van Gogh. It marked the decisive break with tradition and the first step in the passage from the external dimension of sense perception to the inner dimension of the conscious mind.

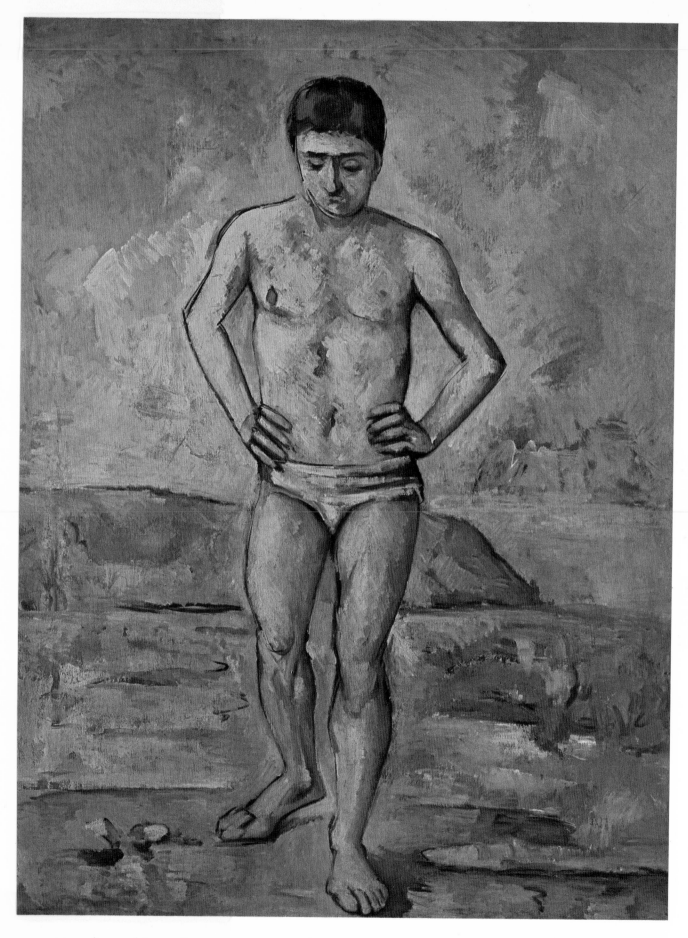

PAUL CÉZANNE (1839-1906). THE LARGE BATHER, 1887-1889. COLLECTION THE MUSEUM OF MODERN ART, NEW YORK.

From 1888 on, adjusting the perspective of his receding planes and consolidating his structural design, Cézanne achieved a monumental synthesis of all the elements that enter into visual perception. His experience of Impressionism had been of great importance as leading him to treat volumes as colored masses, not as shaded reliefs; but he bound those masses into a more tightly knit composition than the Impressionists had ever done. "Cézanne," wrote Signac, "by breaking up colors into their various elements and juxtaposing them in square, clear-cut touches, unconcerned about imitation or adroitness, came closer to the methodical division *practised by the Neo-Impressionists." Actually Cézanne did not break up colors in order to increase the light intensity, but Signac's observation is correct as regards the methodical, cerebral character which the procedure assumed in the hands of Cézanne.*

How very important Impressionism had been for them all is shown not only by the theories Signac put forward but by the pictures he painted, Les Andelys, *for example, in which he raises the horizon line in order to obtain a more compact surface for the shimmer of light vibrations. It is shown above all by Seurat's pictures, less schematic certainly, but freer in the play of fancy; their equally methodical and painstaking organization does not prevent Seurat from achieving the most delicate effects of transparency, as in the studies for the* Grande Jatte, *and a buoyant flow of decorative rhythms, as in the subsequent studies for* Les Poseuses.

Light remained a prime concern of painters. Indeed, after the impressionist period the rendering of light effects became increasingly elaborate following the transformation of visual appearances and spatial representation. After passing through a period of crisis in the 1880s, his so-called "harsh period," Renoir regained all his natural freedom and felicity of handling and built up now semi-abstract forms with precise, rhythmically articulated planes—but planes which, at the same time, float lightly, immersed as they are in a vibrant atmosphere that breaks up contours and softens and modifies forms.

With Degas, bodies were elongated and tapered, disposed in improbable postures. The subtlety of his colors, by drawing out lines, forbade him to linger over descriptive details and modified appearances by modifying space. Lautrec's art breathes the same spirit of synthesis, though he was impelled by different intentions and a temper which, while equally aristocratic and elegant, was more ironic. Thanks to incisive line-work and large, unbounded areas of flat color, his pictures make a direct and forcible appeal to the eye; they bring us face to face with a world observed without pity but also without any innuendo or moralizing.

PAUL SIGNAC (1863-1935). LES ANDELYS: THE BATHS, 1886. COLLECTION OF MAITRE BELLIER, PARIS.

GEORGES SEURAT (1859-1891). STUDY FOR "LA GRANDE JATTE," 1884-1885. THE METROPOLITAN MUSEUM OF ART, NEW YORK.

GEORGES SEURAT (1859-1891). SEATED MODEL, IN PROFILE (SKETCH FOR "LES POSEUSES"), 1887. LOUVRE, PARIS.

AUGUSTE RENOIR (1841-1919). GIRL TYING UP HER HAIR, 1892-1895. PRIVATE COLLECTION.

EDGAR DEGAS (1834-1917). AFTER THE BATH, ABOUT 1895. PASTEL AND WATERCOLOR. COURTAULD INSTITUTE OF ART, LONDON.

HENRI DE TOULOUSE-LAUTREC (1864-1901). MODEL RESTING, 1896. PRIVATE COLLECTION.

PAUL CÉZANNE (1839-1906). PORTRAIT OF JOACHIM GASQUET, 1896-1897. NATIONAL GALLERY, PRAGUE.

III

THE DIMENSION
OF THE MIND

THE LAMP OF TRUTH

To misrepresent the truth was for Ruskin to dishonor poetry and painting. Sacrifice, truth, power, beauty, life, memory and obedience are the "seven lamps of architecture," and their light should clear the mind of cant and artifice—the mind not only of the architect but of the painter and the craftsman as well. Ruskin's moral imperative had both mystical and social foundations; with him the religion of beauty was not a form of aestheticism; its motives were deeply rooted in the conscious mind. Beauty alone can restore its full dignity to human labor and give man joy in his daily tasks. Art is one of the good things of life to which all men have a rightful claim. This being granted, absolute sincerity of expression and procedure becomes for the artist a norm of behavior. It is impossible to attain to beauty, which is a moral category, by concealing the means and materials employed to produce it. In his *Modern Painters* Ruskin asserts that the ideas of beauty are a matter of moral perception, not of intellectual perception. Their source he sought in communion with nature, which he held to be indispensable to artistic creation, though by communion with nature he did not mean imitation of nature. For imitation concerns only the husk and shell of material things; truth, on the contrary, relates to the quality of those things, to the emotions, impressions and thoughts they give rise to. As Ruskin himself put it: "Ideas of truth are the foundation and ideas of imitation the destruction of all art."

This view is an essential component—though not the only one—of the artistic culture of the nineteenth century and entered directly into the vital renewal of art theory and practice which was brought about by William Morris. Ruskin's ideas are sometimes contradictory, but such contradictions are already implicit in the Romantic view of art and in the idealistic historicism of the nineteenth century; they in no way lessen the force of his affirmation of the moral value of art over and above the fluctuations of taste. Refusing to consider the work of art as an isolated entity, Ruskin placed it within its historical context; he made moreover a fundamental distinction between what we see and what we know. "The perception of solid Form is entirely a matter of experience," he wrote. "We *see* nothing but flat colours; and it is only by a series of experiments that we find out that a stain of black or grey indicates the dark side of a solid substance, or that a faint hue indicates that the object in which it appears is far away. The whole technical power of painting depends on our recovery of what may be called the *innocence of the eye*; that is to say, of a sort of childish perception of these flat stains of colour, merely as such, without consciousness of what they signify,—as a blind man would see them if suddenly ifted with sight." E. H. Gombrich, who quotes this passage in *Art and Illusion* (1960), points out that Ruskin's notion of perception derives from the ideas set forth a hundred years earlier by Bishop Berkeley in his *New Theory of Vision*. But it was Ruskin, Gombrich goes on to say, who "posed the problem of painting, and it was this theory that made Roger Fry hail impressionism as the final discovery of appearances."

While Roger Fry—preceded by George Moore—was the enthusiastic apostle of Impressionism in England, Ruskin, in defiance of his own theories, was not even capable of understanding a painter like Whistler. In 1878 Whistler brought his famous libel action against Ruskin for the criticisms published in *Fors Clavigera*. One of Whistler's nocturnes exhibited at the Grosvenor Gallery had been denounced by Ruskin in good set terms, concluding with the remark that he "never expected to hear a coxcomb ask two hundred guineas for flinging a pot of paint in the public's face." At the trial, when the opposing counsel said, "The labor of two days, then, is that for which you ask two hundred guineas?" Whistler retorted, "No, I ask it for the knowledge of a lifetime." The fact is that in this controversy, as G. C. Argan has pointed out, "Whistler was defending Ruskin against Ruskin himself, defending his perfect ideal of transcendence against the fetishism of the painter's craft, his intuitive grasp of a new value of reality against his conventional naturalism, his idea of beauty against his error of taste. And in setting up against an art whose social implications are conveyed through the effective and exemplary presence of the artist, the idea of an art whose social significance is implicit in the work itself as a pure value, Whistler had rectified the error which threatened to nullify Ruskin's vital contribution to that artistic culture which, born in France, bade fair to spread throughout Europe." Whistler in effect reminded his opponent that the Ruskin who sprang to the defense of the Pre-Raphaelites was the Ruskin who had opposed Turner to Claude Lorrain.

Actually the consonance of Ruskin's ideas with those of the Pre-Raphaelites was more apparent than real. Founded in 1848, the Pre-Raphaelite Brotherhood—as they called themselves—included seven artists: Dante Gabriel Rossetti and his brother William Michael, William Holman Hunt, John Everett Millais, Frederic George Stephens, James Collinson, and the sculptor Thomas Woolner. Though he never joined the movement, Ford Madox Brown was profoundly influenced by it. A few years later several of these men, particularly D. G. Rossetti and Madox Brown, were associated with William Morris. What was it that attracted Ruskin to the Pre-Raphaelites? First of all they shared his idealized view of the Middle Ages as an epoch of purity, freedom and sincerity as opposed to the Renaissance and the subsequent imitation of Renaissance canons—an imitation "compounded of indolence, infidelity, sensuality, and shallow pride." Feeling that the painters who came after Raphael were insincere and out of touch with the reality of nature, the Pre-Raphaelites advocated a return to the simple naturalism of the Italian Primitives. "If they adhere to their principles," wrote Ruskin, "and paint nature as it is around them, with the help of modern science, with the earnestness of the men of the thirteenth and fourteenth centuries, they will, as I said, found a new and noble school in England. If their sympathies with the early artists lead them into mediaevalism or romanism, they will of course come to nothing."

The Pre-Raphaelites are a good example of the nineteenth-century taste for reviving some aspect of the past. But they were not eclectics. Their colors were markedly brighter than those of the classical tradition, and the linear patterning of their compositions had a symbolic character which contributed to the rise of English symbolic ornamentalism. But where intrinsic artistic value and style are concerned the Pre-Raphaelites cannot be said to have produced anything as fine or novel as the two great English masters of the early nineteenth century, Constable and Turner, whose work looked towards the future and contributed to shaping the modern sensibility. The painting of the Pre-Raphaelites appears rather to mark the final stage of a tradition of purism, and Turner was certainly closer to the ideals of Ruskin than was John Everett Millais, for example. Most Pre-Raphaelite pictures are marred by literary intentions, the unity and autonomy of the work are impaired, and its literary or symbolic overtones require for their support an infusion of poetry, or poeticalness, which is necessarily extra-pictorial. These pictures are nevertheless an example—and, as it proved, an influential example, both in England and abroad—of a moral commitment, of sound and careful working methods, of a deliberate choice of motifs originating in the mind and not in mere sensation. Ruskin's defense of the Pre-Raphaelites is understandable, even on the strength of that reference to modern science—meaning the natural sciences—which he included in their program but which in reality already formed part of his own theories, as shown by the drawings he made himself in studying the hidden structure of nature.

William Morris's views on art derive from Ruskin's, but Morris had greater powers of organization and his approach to the problems raised by art was more direct and practical. He was introduced to Ruskin's writings by Burne-Jones when they were at Oxford together. Attracted by the Anglo-Catholic movement launched by Newman and the Tractarians, he had thoughts at first of becoming a priest, then gave up the idea, feeling that through art he could better realize the religious vocation, and realize it on a more human level. (There is a curious parallel here to the case of Van Gogh.) From the very start Morris considered the artist as a purveyor of culture, a kind of missionary called upon to live among men and open their eyes to the unfading beauty of the world; he thereby implicitly vindicated the dignity of the work to which the artist sets his hand. In 1856 at the age of twenty-two, while still an undergraduate, he founded and edited the *Oxford and Cambridge Magazine*, for which he secured contributions from Rossetti; this was the origin of the close friendship which sprang up between the two men. That same year, after taking his B. A. degree, he articled himself to George Edmund Street, one of the leading architects of the Gothic Revival, who had been a pupil of Sir George Gilbert Scott. In Street's offices he received a thorough technical grounding, and there he met Philip Webb, who became a lifelong friend of Morris's and designed and built for him the Red House at Upton, Kent.

Morris worked hard but not exclusively at architecture; already a firm believer in the unity of the arts, he painted and carved and made himself a master of the techniques involved. Rossetti advised him to devote himself to painting, and for a time he did so. Under Rossetti's influence he took at once to bright colors in reaction against the dark and dingy tones then prevalent in painting. Burne-Jones was fired by Morris's enthusiasm and stimulated by his tremendous capacity for work and his organizing ability. One of his closest friends and collaborators, he illustrated Morris's books and designed hangings and stained glass for the firm of decorators which Morris founded in 1861. Visiting the Gothic cathedrals of northern France together in 1855, the two men had deplored the restorations to which many of the monuments were being subjected; they shared with Ruskin the conviction that the ancient fabric should be left intact as far as possible. After coming down from Oxford they lived together in London, in Red Lion Square, and both collaborated with Rossetti on the ill-fated frescoes in the Oxford Union. Morris himself soon abandoned easel painting but was ceaselessly active both as a writer and designer; here he found his true vocation. He made no distinction between major and minor arts, maintaining that quality is independent of purpose. The conditions of the applied arts being what they were, Morris followed a different path from that of Sir Henry Cole and Owen Jones. He sought to raise the standards of workmanship in the applied arts; herein lay his greatness and at the same time his limitation. His limitation because history was moving inevitably in another direction; his greatness because he considered the problem not only from the angle of production techniques but from a more general viewpoint, as a problem whose solution lay in bringing about a new awareness of all that is involved in the artistic process. Art he saw not as one component in a page of history written and rewritten by genius alone, but as the everyday activity of artists and craftsmen, the activity of men, not of heroes. He thought of architecture as the product of a union of the arts in which each element was coordinated and harmonized with all the others. "In Europe," he said, "the existence of the other arts is bound up with that of architecture."

In 1859 Morris married Jane Burden and commissioned Philip Webb to build the Red House, an embodiment of all his principles—simple, spacious and functional in its layout, sincere (in accordance with Ruskin's ideas) in the undisguised plainness of its red brick exterior, medievalizing in some details, but with nothing ostentatious about it. Morris himself designed the furniture, and also the decorations in collaboration with Rossetti, Burne-Jones and Ford Madox Brown. The Red House is a landmark in Morris's career. There, for the five years he occupied it (1860-1865), his friends forgathered and talked over their plans and ideas; it was the ideal setting for his own work and a demonstration of what could be done in the way of furnishing, decoration and house design. The work on the Red House moreover had suggested a fresh activity, beyond the personal sphere, and in 1861 the firm of Morris, Marshall, Faulkner & Co., "Fine Art Workmen in Painting, Carving, Furniture and the Metals," opened its offices in London. Ford Madox Brown, D. G. Rossetti, Burne-Jones and Philip Webb were associated with the firm, with Morris in charge. The prospectus they issued announced that they were prepared to undertake church and house decoration, carving, stained glass, metal work, wallpapers, hangings, chintzes and carpets.

Morris founded his firm as a protest against commercialism, mass production, and the cheapening of taste which they were causing; as a plea in favor of natural decoration, pure color, and a spirit of beauty unadulterated by ostentation. While most of the designs and cartoons were supplied by Rossetti, Burne-Jones, Webb and Madox Brown, Morris himself took a hand in the work, chose the colors, and mastered the various crafts. Many difficulties had to be overcome, first of all the difficulty of reconciling Morris's democratic ideal, his desire to bring beautiful things within the reach of all, with the high cost of his handmade goods; for he was not the man to lower his costs by lowering the quality of the material or the workmanship. In 1862 the firm showed its work at the International Exhibition in London and was awarded two gold medals. In 1867 it was commissioned to decorate the dining room in the South Kensington Museum; here Morris intervened personally and, judging part of the work to be unsatisfactory, had it done over again. In 1874, for financial reasons, Morris, Marshall, Faulkner & Co. was dissolved and restarted under the name of Morris & Co., with Morris as sole manager and the continued collaboration of Burne-Jones and Philip Webb. The firm's activities were carried on with renewed enthusiasm, the sale of its wallpapers and chintzes enabling Morris to supply fine products at reasonable prices.

Morris was simplifying his designs under the influence of Oriental motifs and also, as Peter Floud has noted, of Italian Renaissance tapestries. This goes to show how in actual practice he overcame the limitations of Ruskin's taste and the imagery of the Pre-Raphaelites. Floud has divided the designs for chintzes into four periods: naturalistic (1872-1876), symmetrical (1876-1883), diagonal (1883-1890), and again naturalistic (1890-1896) but now with greater clarity in the patterning. Morris printed his materials by hand and made his own dyes, at which he arrived after several years of experimentation. "These researches were to such good effect," writes Philip Henderson, "that today the colors of some Morris fabrics are as good as when they first emerged from the dye-vat. In most cases they have actually improved with washing and the passage of time." After 1890 he applied the knowledge and experience of a lifetime to a new field of activity: typography and printing. He designed new type faces, defined the ornamentation of the printed book with respect to its content, and conceived its beauty in accordance with the principle of an architectonic layout. That beauty, he felt, depended on a page make-up and type face which did not tire the eye, on high-quality, carefully chosen inks, and on the spacing of the letters. He worked out the proportions of the page layout, maintaining that it must be judged in relation to the two facing pages, not merely the single page. In Kelmscott Manor on the upper Thames, which he had bought in 1871, he set up a private printing press and in 1891 the first volume, his own *Story of the Glittering Plain*, issued from the Kelmscott Press; it was followed by many others, notably the *Golden Legend* and the great Kelmscott Chaucer. These beautiful books were the crowning achievement of a life devoted to the upholding of moral and aesthetic values. Morris died on the 3rd of October 1896, at the age of sixty-two.

Morris was no enemy of progress; what he struggled against all his life was an indiscriminate progress unaccompanied by moral and social improvement. His socialism, less utopian than Ruskin's, sprang from his intense desire to see the birth of a new social order in which art would not be relegated to the level of a useless, parasitic activity, not be cut off from its roots which must lie in the social fabric itself. His revival of the handicrafts and the community ideals of the Middle Ages was undoubtedly a limiting factor in the effective spread of his influence, but he did impress upon a whole generation the necessity of bringing art into the daily life of all classes of society; and here his influence was momentous. Even in his lifetime his teaching bore fruit: in 1882 Arthur H. Mackmurdo founded the Century Guild for the applied arts, and in 1884 the Art Workers' Guild was formed. Nikolaus Pevsner has pointed out that the first result of Morris's teaching was to awaken interest in a field —the arts of design and handicraft—which had been almost entirely neglected. At the Arts and Crafts Exhibition Society, founded in 1888, Morris showed his own products and exerted a direct influence on the younger artists: Walter Crane, who was closely associated with the work at the Kelmscott Press and designed socialist posters; and C. R. Ashbee, C. F. A. Voysey and W. R. Lethaby, all outstanding designers and architects, active not only in their chosen fields but also as teachers. These artists released themselves from the thrall of the past and turned their back on the Middle Ages in order to "live and work in the present," as Voysey put it. Machinery for them was not a destructive force but a reality which has to be coped with and bent to man's use and advantage. These were the men who in England forged the link between the hopes and experiences of the nineteenth century and the performances of the twentieth.

William Morris set little store by the possibilities of painting; after a time easel pictures ceased to interest him, and he suggested to Burne-Jones, who continued to paint in the Pre-Raphaelite manner, that they should devote themselves to decoration. Rossetti remained his master in all that regarded painting, but in the long run the literary inspiration of the Pre-Raphaelites, their idealized picture of the Middle Ages, failed to satisfy him. In his stained-glass windows, like the three with angel musicians which Morris designed for Morris, Marshall, Faulkner & Co. between 1872 and 1874, the figure itself is in the Pre-Raphaelite style, but the stylized plant forms in the surrounding panes depart from the manner of both Rossetti and Burne-Jones. He drew even further away from his friends in designing the patterns of his printed textiles; these, printed by hand from wooden blocks, required the utmost clarity of design and a radical simplification of motifs. The "Daffodil" chintz, the last chintz designed by Morris, in 1891, is one of the best examples. Such works as Rossetti's Sir Galahad *and Burne-Jones's* Golden Stairs *remain somewhat constricted by their medieval or early Renaissance inspiration. For Morris, on the other hand, the Middle Ages served as a term of reference that was more ideological than ideal, and therefore did not cramp his style.*

The artist, then, felt called upon to contribute to the beauty and amenity of the setting in which men live their lives; but he made that contribution on his own terms, without any compromise. Whistler, unlike Morris, took not the slightest interest in the social aspects of art, but he felt it his duty as an artist to uphold good taste and, if need be, impose it on others. The story of the "Peacock Room" is significant. At the request of a wealthy English shipowner and art patron, Frederick R. Leyland, it was originally designed by two architects, Shaw and Jeckyll, who probably bore in mind the room decorated by Morris and his associates in the South Kensington Museum. It was a dining room in which were to be placed a set of blue and white porcelain and a painting by Whistler, his Princess of the Land of Porcelain *of 1864. But when Whistler saw the room he insisted on redecorating it entirely. He threw out the Spanish leather hanging with which Jeckyll had covered the walls, changed the color scheme, emphasized the exotic note, added his peacock panels, and put his signature to the room as to a picture—to the dismay of both architects and owner. "Pictures," he pronounced, "have been painted often enough without consideration of the room in which they were to hang; in this case I have painted a room to harmonize with my picture." Triumphing over all opposition, Whistler solved the problem from a painter's point of view and, as in some of his pictures, created a "harmony in blue and gold."*

WILLIAM MORRIS (1834-1896). WOMAN PLAYING A LUTE, 1872-1874. STAINED GLASS. VICTORIA AND ALBERT MUSEUM, LONDON.

WILLIAM MORRIS (1834-1896). THE "DAFFODIL" CHINTZ, 1891. VICTORIA AND ALBERT MUSEUM, LONDON.

DANTE GABRIEL ROSSETTI (1828-1882). SIR GALAHAD, 1864. BY COURTESY OF THE TRUSTEES, TATE GALLERY, LONDON.

EDWARD BURNE-JONES (1833-1898). THE GOLDEN STAIRS, 1880. BY COURTESY OF THE TRUSTEES, TATE GALLERY, LONDON.

JAMES MCNEILL WHISTLER (1834-1903). THE PEACOCK ROOM. FINISHED IN 1877.
BY COURTESY OF THE SMITHSONIAN INSTITUTION, FREER GALLERY OF ART, WASHINGTON, D.C.

TANGIBLE FORM

Impressionist painting was altogether free from anything in the way of metaphysics or intellectual speculation. The reaction against Impressionism which developed in France after about 1885 was on the contrary based on an accentuation of the symbolic significance of images; it was a conscious attempt to give artistic expression an intellectual content. For the representation of nature, for the recording of sense impressions and the emotions kindled by them, the Neo-Impressionists substituted the representation of an idea; in effect they extended the artist's field of inquiry and inspiration from the observation of external phenomena to the consideration of motifs and suggestions impinging on the conscious mind. In the Symbolist Manifesto which he published in *Le Figaro* on September 18, 1886, Jean Moréas asserted that "the idea must be clothed in tangible form." Moréas was referring to poetry, but Symbolism by its very character offered an aesthetic applicable to all forms of artistic expression, and one that particularly appealed to painters and sculptors. As Rodin said: "Look at the masterpieces of art. All their beauty comes from the mind." All the art that followed Impressionism was affected by Symbolism, and not in France alone.

There were of course precedents for all this. Impressionism itself represented if not a reaction at least a deviation from the Romantic outlook. But contemporaneously with Impressionism, or just before it, there had been other groups and other painters whose work was in a typically Romantic vein, with clearly symbolic overtones. The painting of the Pre-Raphaelites is an example in England; in France the work of Gustave Moreau, Puvis de Chavannes and Odilon Redon (who was born in the same year as Monet) anticipated Symbolism in many ways, though each of these men followed a path of his own. Gustave Moreau was attracted by esoteric myths, but his literary inspiration was always in harmony with the pictorial means he employed; indeed it was dominated by his rich, elaborately wrought pigments. It is of some significance surely that painters like Matisse and Rouault were trained in Moreau's studio. "The rise of his art," as Germain Bazin has observed, "coincides with the publication of *Salammbô*... Here we have a most remarkable example of literary and artistic synchronism." And Manet's *Déjeuner sur l'herbe* and *Olympia* appeared within a year of Flaubert's novel.

Puvis de Chavannes was attracted by another myth, that of a metaphysical humanism, an untroubled Arcadia, literary no doubt but rigorously delineated in all the purity of his pictorial and plastic means. Both the works of Gustave Moreau and those, however different, of Puvis de Chavannes are the fruit of a purely mental inspiration, the concrete illustration of imaginative experience; they are decorations in the sense that they evade any implication beyond what is inherent in the pictorial process. Moreau may have seen some of the work of the Pre-Raphaelites, who exhibited at the Paris World's Fair of 1855. "While the 1855 exhibition marked the triumph of romanticism (Delacroix), Ingrism (Ingres) and naturalism (Courbet)," writes Germain Bazin, "this English group alone showed paintings based on ideas." And the influence of the Pre-Raphaelites was probably felt by Puvis de Chavannes as well. Even so, both Puvis and Moreau were typical products of the artistic culture of nineteenth-century France, for each in his own way conveyed in concrete pictorial terms his literary inspiration and metaphysical ideals. Cézanne reproached Puvis de Chavannes for purveying second-rate literature. It is difficult to draw a parallel between two such painters as Puvis and Cézanne, for the latter is one of those masters who appear but once in a century or two and change the whole course of art history; his judgment here, nevertheless, is quite unfair. An academic Romantic Puvis may have been, and a painter of limited gifts, but he restored a fundamental simplicity to the painter's means, he worked out a clear and rational schema of composition, and indeed this was his prime concern, as we know from a statement of Puvis's recorded by Maurice Denis. "For every clear idea there is a plastic conception which will convey it... I turn that conception over and over in my mind until I have clarified it and it appears to me in the sharpest possible outline. Then I look for a scene and figures which will fit it exactly. This, if you like, is symbolism."

Odilon Redon, who was a great admirer of Gustave Moreau, also worked along symbolist lines but his sources of inspiration were very different. The metaphysical symbolism of Puvis de Chavannes was based on nature; he took the figures and objects of the visible world and integrated them into a flat linear pattern in which they seem to stand apart in a serene and timeless realm where nothing ever happens. For Redon naturalism was the enemy of art; he reproached the Impressionists for having confined themselves to the observation of the natural world, for it was this, he held, that has prevented the artist from exploring the unconscious mind and giving shape to ideas, dreams and fancies. As early as 1874, the year of the first group exhibition of the Impressionists, Redon published a set of lithographs entitled, significantly enough, *Dans le rêve*, and clearly symbolist in inspiration. Redon painted dream images and figments of the unconscious; he did not exhibit them in the light of reason and conventional logic but veiled in the shimmering colors of his own aesthetic of ambiguity and indetermination. "All can be done by docile submission to the uprush of the unconscious," he wrote. And again: "Painting is not mere representation of three-dimensional forms, but human beauty adorned with the prestige of thought." Hostile to what he considered the materialism of the Impressionists, Redon defined his painting in terms of a color and light which—though in fact not very far removed from those of impressionist painting—were invested by him with the potent symbols of his inner life. With color and light he laid bare the mysteries of a world unseen but glimpsed in dreams and fancies.

Impressionism was unquestionably the most important, most modern art revolution of the nineteenth century, but the work of Moreau, Puvis de Chavannes and Redon also contributed to the shaping of a modern sensibility. While both Matisse and Rouault were trained under Moreau, who through them exerted an indirect influence on the Fauve movement, the purism of Puvis de Chavannes attracted Picasso and the Surrealists paid tribute to Odilon Redon. These three artists were the immediate precursors of the symbolist movement, and were recognized as such in the last two decades of the century when they were still active. Symbolism, however, has so many contrasting aspects that it is difficult to mark out a uniform line of development and impossible to reduce its various manifestations to a common denominator. The avowed aim of representing ideas is in fact insufficient for us to lay down any general rule; that aim lent itself in practice to too many different interpretations in the field of painting. Bonnard, Vuillard, Maurice Denis, and all the Nabis, undoubtedly worked within the ambit of the symbolist aesthetic, yet they were the very men who rejected the facile admixture of painting and literature; and it was Maurice Denis who in 1890 "uttered one of the great battle-cries of modern art," the most forthright affirmation so far of the autonomy of the painter's craft and idiom, when he said: "Remember that a picture, before being a war-horse, a nude woman or some kind of anecdote, is essentially a flat surface covered with colors arranged in a certain order."

With Gauguin, with the Nabis, with Van Gogh in particular, art became something very different from the things that meet the eye in the visible world: it bodied forth emotions, ideas, moods and states of mind. Outside France, however, Symbolism very often lapsed into a form of naturalism. There were many painters and above all decorators who, drawing on a literary or indeed wholly intellectual source of inspiration, proceeded to interpret it in terms of rhythms borrowed from visual appearances. The Italian Divisionists, for example, while following the lead of Seurat and Signac, were concerned with bringing out the symbolic implications of natural images. But the consequences of this lack of clarity and coherence became most evident in the decoration of objects, in interior decoration generally, and even in architecture. In this field valid results were obtained only when naturalistic ornamentalism was kept well under control or was absent altogether, as in the sound and coherent designs of men like Horta, Van de Velde and Mackintosh, of Gallé and Tiffany—those men, in a word, who did not give way to that extravagant fluency of design, typical of so much of Art Nouveau, in which decoration tended to run riot.

146

The important thing to note is that in the last two decades of the nineteenth century the temper of the art world, the frame of mind of the artists themselves, had radically changed: the expressive felicity of Impressionism had given place to uneasiness and uncertainty. Van Gogh and Gauguin are the most striking examples of this change of temper, but it reached its highest pitch in the work of Toulouse-Lautrec; with him the spontaneous scrutiny of the Impressionists was transformed into a mentally controlled process. "I have tried to see things truly, not ideally," wrote Lautrec in a letter of 1881. But to see things truly no longer meant surrendering to the emotions aroused by nature, it meant discovering, eliciting the face of a reality which might well be cruel and pitiless. In his paintings and drawings, in his lithographs and posters, Lautrec delineated figures by a skillful use of contour lines which synthesize planes, which assert the priority of style over the immediate analytical rendering of naturalistic detail, its priority too over any excessive idealization. Far though he was from Impressionism, with which however he was very well acquainted, particularly through the works of Manet and Renoir, Lautrec profited by its spirit of synthesis, substituting for descriptive analysis a conciseness and trenchancy which enabled him to sum up not only the physiognomy but the character of his figures with a few deft strokes, direct lighting and broad areas of flat color. The elegance of his line undoubtedly has a decorative value very much in the Art Nouveau manner, but it is not an evasion into the mythological world of the Decadents; it is very far indeed from the symbol-ridden neurosis and decorative extravagance of artists like Toorop, for example. Lautrec in fact belonged to the great tradition of French draftsmanship which had spanned the entire century, from David to Degas by way of Ingres, and which in Toulouse-Lautrec found its culminating expression.

The rankling uneasiness that had crept into art sprang from the desire for deeper insights, the effort to penetrate beyond appearances, and the impossibility of establishing an equipollent relationship with the world. Deepened insights do not lead back to nature, nor are they yielded by positive science, which was in any case about to be challenged by the new science. Albert Aurier, one of the first critics to grasp the significance of the painting of Gauguin and Van Gogh, assured artists that positive science would only lead them back to the purely animal state and on this account roundly condemned Impressionism as being no more than "the representation of material appearances."

It was Aurier who in 1891, in a famous article in the *Mercure de France*, laid down the five fundamental principles of symbolist painting. "The work of art," he announced, "will be (1) *ideational*, for its unique ideal will be the expression of ideas; (2) *symbolist*, for it will express ideas through forms; (3) *synthetic*, for it will set down these forms, these signs, in such a way as to make them generally comprehensible; (4) *subjective*, for the object will not be represented for its own sake but as signifying the idea perceived by the subject; (5) it will accordingly be *decorative*, for decorative painting properly so called, as practised by the Egyptians, and very probably by the Greeks and the Primitives, is nothing else but an art form at once subjective, synthetic, symbolist and ideational."

Aurier's symbolist art was closely akin to the symbolist poetry of Jean Moréas, but the synthetism he looked forward to derived directly from Gauguin, who had been airing his views and illustrating them in his paintings for several years past. Even so, Gauguin's synthesis was above all a synthesis of sensations, emotions, ideas and moods, and this was the means whereby he transcribed on canvas the total impact of emotional experience. He considered the painting not as a confession or a release, but as an autonomous object embodying the very condition of existence, not an allegorical representation of it. With Gauguin the notion of catharsis was banished from art for good. In this respect too he stands apart from and indeed opposed to Impressionism—which had nevertheless exerted a decisive influence on him. But the scrutiny of nature and natural structures was of little use in carrying out an investigation into the workings of the mind, the layers of consciousness deposited by the worldly experience of the individual. Sensations remained for Gauguin the primary basis of knowledge—thought came afterwards—but they could not be confined to merely visual sensations. Painting in his hands did not produce an illusion, did not imitate visual appearances, did not offer the beholder something which already formed part of his optical experience. Figures cast no shadows, colors are remote from those of nature, harmonies result from contrasts and not from concordances. Emile Bernard claimed that he was the first to use those thick contour lines which gave rise to the Cloisonnism of Gauguin; but what for Bernard was a technical device for consolidating natural forms became in Gauguin's hands a means of subverting normal vision and emphasizing his rejection of empirical observation.

"Do not copy nature too closely," warned Gauguin. "Art is an abstraction. Draw it out of nature by dreaming before her." But Gauguin's dreams were no haven of refuge; they were troubled dreams, and the "magnetic current of thought" aroused in him a sense of otherworldliness, just as it did, perhaps even more dramatically, in Van Gogh. The idea of death raised the problem of a new relationship, it crept into his work and upset its stylistic balance. How was he to arrive at an image of that idea, at a space and time such as might sum it up? These had to be evoked and elicited from the same indistinct commotions, and not through the "magic casements" of Odilon Redon but through a complete subversion of the rules which for centuries had governed unchallenged the art of pictorial representation. "A treetrunk whose local color is bluish grey becomes pure blue," he said, because a tree is an emotion, not only a sensation; because it is a synthesis of successive moments of existence, not a poetic description of an instant of perception. "I have always thought," wrote Gauguin, "that the painter's poetry is something special, and not the illustration and translation of writings by way of forms." A direct poetry, calling for deep-seated inspirations and boundless horizons, a primordial, pristine force, a world in which sensation is unmodified by custom and habit. No wonder, then, that Gauguin forsook a civilization in which only material values seemed to triumph and went in search of that world, first in Brittany, then in Martinique, finally in the South Seas. That quest was not an evasion or a flight from reality; it offered him rather an opportunity of coming to grips with the myth that haunted him and experiencing it not as some vague literary and academic aspiration, but as a reality.

Gauguin gathered around him a whole group of artists at Pont-Aven and Le Pouldu in Brittany. Following his advice and under his supervision, Paul Sérusier in 1888 painted a small landscape exemplifying the principles of Symbolism and Synthetism which he called *The Talisman*. Back in Paris, Sérusier showed it to his friends at the Académie Jullian, Maurice Denis, Pierre Bonnard, Paul Ranson, and Henri-Gabriel Ibels. Together with Ker-Xavier Roussel and Edouard Vuillard, these young painters formed the group which the poet Cazalis christened the Nabis (from the Hebrew word meaning prophet); in time it came to include René Piot, Félix Vallotton, Jan Verkade, the Hungarian painter Rippl-Ronai, and the sculptors Georges Lacombe and Aristide Maillol. The activity of most of these artists extended far into the twentieth century, but the works they produced and the theories they set forth in the 1890s belong entirely to the symbolist movement and were influenced by the mystical and esoteric thought of that day, and by Japanese prints. All of them however—and this was the lesson they learned from Gauguin—took for granted the autonomy of the artist's means of expression. "Art," wrote Maurice Denis, the theorist of the group, "is before all else a means of expression, a creation of our mind for which nature is only the pretext." And he distinguished between "mystical and allegorical tendencies, meaning expression in terms of the subject, and symbolic tendencies, meaning expression in terms of the work of art." This sense of the autonomy of art led the Nabis to seek the fundamental unity underlying all manifestations of art. They were painters and sculptors, they designed stage sets, posters, book and magazine illustrations, stained-glass windows. Art is necessary to society and it is the artist's duty, they felt, to bring his talents to bear in as many fields as possible. They welcomed art in all its forms and contrasts. Thus they not only admired Gauguin but sought to remold the ideological unity of the various trends of expression represented by painters as different as Redon, Puvis, Moreau, Lautrec, Van Gogh and Cézanne. Modern art for the Nabis was not an oddity or a digression, but the stuff of history itself.

THE MYTH

The myth may be classical or romantic (like the sabbath in Faust*), pagan or Christian. Nearly always it is an evasion, a flight from reality. Courbet had refused to paint angels on the plea that he had never seen any. But when literature made its way into painting it became possible to paint almost anything, seen or unseen—but usually with an ambiguity prejudicial to the autonomy of the painter's means of expression. Puvis de Chavannes and Gustave Moreau, however, proved capable of adapting the myth, classical and Christian in the first, esoteric in the second, to the peculiar conditions of the painter's medium, Puvis with an exemplary rigor of design, Moreau with his richly textured pigments. Puvis's Arcadia and Moreau's Salome (a figure dear to the Decadents, to Aubrey Beardsley and Oscar Wilde) found in painting their modern incarnation. Where the two French painters succeeded, Böcklin and Hodler failed. With the first mythology became a romantic, sentimental effusion; with the second, a pretext for abstract decoration, without space, in which an ascetic purity and Christian intentions cannot dispel the tedium of a Nordic saga. These are cases in which painting has evaded the critical issues of history and passed into a metaphysical vacuum where it could not possibly thrive.*

Albert Pinkham Ryder was the most visionary of the American painters of the late nineteenth century; less refined, but with far greater power, his vision has much in common with Moreau's. The myth of the poet, transcending the image which represents him, is conveyed in the rich disarray of the pigments, whose rugged texture, by his own admission, later caught the eye of Jackson Pollock. But it was Redon, Munch and Rodin above all who, never letting themselves be led astray by literature, gave expression in terms of myth to the anxieties and vexations of the contemporary spirit. Opening up a vast field of inquiry, Redon descended into the depths of the mind and brought up a whole world of forms "transposed or transfigured, with no relation to contingent things, yet with a logic of their own." The uncanny poetry of Redon gave way in Munch to a despair which convulses forms and merges painting and being in a single cry of anguish: Munch brings us to the threshold of Expressionism. For Rodin the symbol could be nothing ambiguous; even a fragment, a hand fraught with hidden meanings, had to be given its precise definition as a form, whose allegorical overtones were redeemed by its artistic perfection.

PIERRE PUVIS DE CHAVANNES (1824-1898). SUMMER,
1891. THE CLEVELAND MUSEUM OF ART, J.H. WADE COLLECTION.

ARNOLD BÖCKLIN (1827-1901). ULYSSES AND CALYPSO, 1883. KUNSTMUSEUM, BASEL.

FERDINAND HODLER (1853-1918). THE CHOSEN ONE, 1893-1894. GOTTFRIED KELLER STIFTUNG, BERN
(ON LOAN TO THE KUNSTMUSEUM, BERN).

ALBERT P. RYDER (1847-1917). PEGASUS, OR THE POET ENTERING THE REALM OF THE MUSES, 1887.
OWNED BY THE WORCESTER ART MUSEUM, WORCESTER, MASS.

GUSTAVE MOREAU (1826-1898). THE APPARITION, ABOUT 1875. MUSÉE MOREAU, PARIS.

ODILON REDON (1840-1916). THE DREAM, ABOUT 1904. CLAUDE BLANCPAIN COLLECTION, FRIBOURG, SWITZERLAND.

EDVARD MUNCH (1863-1944). VAMPIRE, ABOUT 1895. DR OTHMAR HUBER COLLECTION, GLARUS, SWITZERLAND.

AUGUSTE RODIN (1840-1917). THE HAND OF GOD, ABOUT 1895. MARBLE. MUSÉE RODIN, PARIS.

GAUGUIN AND THE NABIS

In October 1888 Gauguin left Brittany and joined Van Gogh in Provence—with tragic results. After a violent quarrel, Van Gogh cut off his own ear in a fit of madness and had to be interned in an asylum, while Gauguin beat a hurried retreat to Paris. It was a time of great spiritual tension, but also of great enrichment. In November, shortly before things came to a crisis, both men painted the same scene, the old Roman cemetery of Arles known as Les Alyscamps (Elysii Campi), a short avenue bordered by a few ancient tombs and "carpeted with a thick layer of orange and yellow fallen leaves," as Van Gogh described it in a letter to his brother Theo. Gauguin in his version of Les Alyscamps *made great play with completely arbitrary colors, following the principles he himself had begun to lay down in Brittany at Pont-Aven, then, at Le Pouldu, had carried to extremes in pictures like* Jacob wrestling with the Angel *and the* Yellow Christ. *Even before leaving for Arles he had urged Paul Sérusier to step up his colors to their highest intensity. "How do you see this tree?" he said to Sérusier when they were out painting together. "It's green, you say? Well, then, put down green, the richest green on your palette. And what about that shadow? Rather blue? Don't be afraid to paint it as blue as you possibly can." The resulting picture, a landscape known as* The Talisman, *painted on the lid of a cigar box, transmitted Gauguin's lesson, by way of Sérusier, to the future Nabis.*

When the group was formed in 1889, the Nabis met each week in the Paris studio of Paul Ranson, which they called "The Temple." For they were mystics and formed a kind of brotherhood; one member, Jan Verkade, took holy orders, and another, Maurice Denis, dedicated himself to religious painting. While the example of Gauguin was of fundamental importance for them, especially his use of flat, pure colors with symbolic overtones, they were also influenced by the flat patterning of Japanese prints; Bonnard in fact was called the "Japanese Nabi." Rhythmic composition and flowing linework give their painting a flavor very similar to that of Art Nouveau. Their work has, however, a unity of style unparalleled by that of any other group or movement. It was the artist's duty, according to Maurice Denis, to create symbols capable of conveying emotions, and to do so without slavishly copying the scene before his eyes. In their pictures the Nabis made no concessions to any form of literary description. Though with them painting tended to be a reflection of the mind, it always retained its visual appeal as painting. So true is this that the work of Bonnard, which continued to develop until after the Second World War, is now seen to be one of the most significant and original achievements in the art of our time.

PAUL GAUGUIN (1848-1903). LES ALYSCAMPS, ARLES, 1888. LOUVRE, PARIS.

PAUL SÉRUSIER (1863-1927). THE TALISMAN, 1888. PRIVATE COLLECTION.

MAURICE DENIS (1870–1943). SOIR TRINITAIRE, 1891. COLLECTION OF MADAME P. DÉJEAN, LOUVECIENNES.

PIERRE BONNARD (1867-1947). WOMAN WITH RABBIT, 1891. COLLECTION OF PROFESSOR WILLIAM RUBIN, NEW YORK.

a rigor of design which kept him from lapsing into purely decorative fantasies. Through the functional clarity of his line he had arrived at a style free from the literary inflections of the Pre-Raphaelites and had even gone beyond his own medieval preferences. Those who followed his example did not always show the same rigor or the same concern for essentials. In England however, as attested above all by the work of Mackintosh, his lesson was determinant in this respect: Ashbee, Voysey, even Walter Crane, also Beardsley (who was influenced not only by Burne-Jones but by the books of the Kelmscott Press), were all undoubtedly affected by Symbolism, though they kept the linear patterning of their decorations well under control, never giving way to sentimental effusions. It should not be forgotten that Ashbee and Voysey, like Mackmurdo moreover, were practising architects.

Mackmurdo's starting point was the theoretical position defined by Morris in his writings and exemplified in the stylistic unity of his designs, whether for furniture or book illustrations. The motif on the title page of Mackmurdo's book *Wren's City Churches* is identical with the one on the back of some of the chairs he designed. Inspired by peacock feathers, this motif retains a naturalistic stamp and shows Mackmurdo to be one of the initiators of Art Nouveau; yet, for all its elegance, it serves a definite constructive purpose. Something of the same rather mannered elegance appears in the designs of Walter Crane, though—as in his posters, for example—it is never allowed to detract from their clarity and legibility. There was little danger of this with Crane, for he illustrated many children's books and well understood the importance of simplicity of design and direct visual appeal.

The work of Aubrey Beardsley undoubtedly stands on a higher artistic level. Beardsley was one of the outstanding draftsmen of the late nineteenth century. Resolving volumes into flat patterns, he

ARTHUR H. MACKMURDO (1851-1942).
TITLE PAGE OF "WREN'S CITY CHURCHES," 1883.

JAN TOOROP (1858-1928).
"O GRAVE, WHERE IS THY VICTORY?" 1892.
DRAWING. PRINT ROOM, RIJKSMUSEUM, AMSTERDAM.

WALTER CRANE (1845-1915).
POSTER FOR THE FIRST OF MAY, LONDON, 1895.

AUBREY BEARDSLEY (1872-1898).
ILLUSTRATION FOR OSCAR WILDE'S "SALOME," 1894.

165

EMILE GALLÉ (1846-1904).
BOWL OF CUT AND ENGRAVED CRYSTAL, 1889.
MUSÉE DE L'ÉCOLE DES BEAUX-ARTS, NANCY.

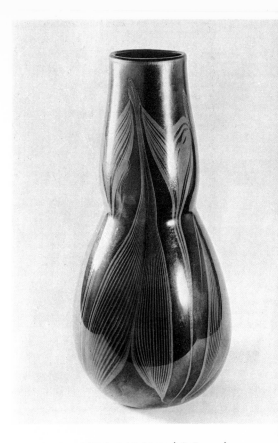

LOUIS C. TIFFANY (1848-1933).
VASE IN THE FORM OF A BOTTLE-GOURD, 1896.
OESTERREICHISCHES MUSEUM FÜR ANGEWANDTE KUNST, V

HENRY VAN DE VELDE (1863-1957). CANDLESTICK, 1902.
NORDENFJELDSKE KUNSTINDUSTRIMUSEUM, TRONDHEIM.

CHARLES R. ASHBEE (1863-1942).
SILVER BOWL, ABOUT 1893.
VICTORIA AND ALBERT MUSEUM, LONDON.

5

SYMBOLIC DECORATION

If the work of art was to fall in line with Symbolism, as Albert Aurier held that it must, everything connected with artistic production would also be inspired by symbolic motifs. The trend that got under way with the Arts and Crafts movement and, by sometimes devious means, gave rise to Art Nouveau, kept almost entirely to the imagery of Symbolism. The symbolist emphasis on "the idea" may be taken as the common denominator of almost all the art forms that appeared in the last fifteen years of the nineteenth century. Behind the posters of the period, from Chéret's to Bonnard's, the style of furniture design and interior decoration, book illustrations and graphic art—behind them all lay Symbolism. For Emile Gallé "symbols are the points at which ideas take concrete form," as he declared in a lecture on "Le Décor Symbolique." All this was at once an advantage and a limitation, for such was the contradictory aspect of Art Nouveau. An advantage because Symbolism provided the means and inspiration for a coherent and distinctive style, both in the so-called major and minor arts; a limitation because, by transforming the idea into allegory (which is what usually happened), Art Nouveau tended to neglect the function of forms in its exclusive concern with abstract decoration.

Morris had shown the way to resolve this dilemma; indeed he himself had overcome it with

VICTOR HORTA (1861-1947). DINING ROOM IN THE HÔTEL HORTA, BRUSSELS, 1900.
BY COURTESY OF THE BARONNE HORTA, BRUSSELS.

CHARLES RENNIE MACKINTOSH (1868-1928).
ENTRANCE HALL OF HILL HOUSE
AT HELENSBURGH, NEAR GLASGOW, 1902-1903.

CHARLES F. A. VOYSEY (1857-1941).
DRAWING ROOM OF THE ARTIST'S HOUSE,
"THE ORCHARD," AT CHORLEY WOOD,
BUCKINGHAM, 1900.

concentrated all the evocative and expressive power of his art on line in conjunction with patches of black. Reduced to an extreme simplicity, his graphic means are handled with an intensity and a narrative skill from which Paul Klee was to learn much. Beardsley stands at the opposite pole from Jan Toorop; both were influenced by Oriental prints, but any similarity in their treatment of sinuous line is more apparent than real. A Dutch artist, Toorop lived both in England and in Belgium, at Brussels, where he was on friendly terms with Verhaeren and Maeterlinck. It was these literary friendships that led him to abandon the Neo-Impressionism of his earlier work in favor of Symbolism. But his line lacks the expressive power of Beardsley's, nor has it the same autonomy; his works always crystallize around a subject or a literary inspiration which he rarely succeeds in lifting to a purely pictorial plane.

Emile Gallé and Louis C. Tiffany, one French, the other American, were the best representatives of that *fin-de-siècle* style which found international expression in interior decorations and furnishings; they were the creators of the elegant refinements of the *belle époque*. Gallé especially owed much to Symbolism, but in neither artist does symbolic linearism impair the fitness of the form. Indeed both deserve credit for the attention they paid to their materials; treating crystal as a noble medium, they bent it to the exigencies of form much as a sculptor bends his materials. The guiding aim which Morris had set himself, to produce high-quality art products available to all, and which hardly thirty years before had seemed illusory, was now to be realized. Morris's teaching at last bore fruit, notably in the work of architects like Ashbee in England and Van de Velde in Belgium, who devoted much of their time to designing objects and furnishings, convinced as they were of the fundamental unity, both stylistic and moral, that underlies all forms of artistic activity.

LINE OF BEAUTY

"The evolution of ideas and the conditions of social life can no longer be accommodated to pictures and statues *alone*. It is folly to rely only on them to provide for our material existence, as it is blindness to suppose that they can satisfy all the artistic needs of our time." So wrote Henry van de Velde in 1893. In Van de Velde we see the influence of Ruskin and Morris still actively at work, but now the new century lay ahead, raising other problems and calling for other solutions. An alienated public had to be wooed back to art, the breach of the recent past to be healed, a style to be worked out for that purpose. Art Nouveau, of which Van de Velde was one of the leading exponents and unquestionably the most lucid theorist, fell heir to the ideological legacy of the nineteenth century which it summed up and voiced, though with many ambiguities, in an attempt to reconcile artistic activity, as an autonomous means of expression, with the demands of social activity. Van de Velde himself was not only a painter who had profited by the example of men like Seurat and Gauguin; he was an architect, a decorator, a graphic artist, and what we would call today a designer, in the strictest sense of the word. Let it not be forgotten, moreover, that he was the immediate predecessor of Gropius on the teaching staff of the Weimar School of Applied Arts.

All the best representatives of Art Nouveau were moved by the conviction that art in all its forms —regardless of outdated academic distinctions between "major" and "minor" arts—must have its roots in modern life, must form an integral part of that life, exploit its technical devices and give them an aesthetic quality. These were the premises which Art Nouveau laid down for the art and culture to come, and in this, rather than its period style and design, lies the significance of its lesson. Of course it was not created out of nothing; on the contrary, it was the outcome and summation of the art trends of the century. While never lapsing into eclecticism, it went far to reconcile its ingredients by developing a strikingly distinctive and unitary style. The cultural and stylistic legacy on which Art Nouveau drew is highly complex and the results, it must be said, are only rarely positive. It was an idiom that varied greatly from country to country, depending on the traditions that nourished it; but whether it was called Art Nouveau or Jugendstil (Germany), Sezessionsstil (Vienna), Stile Liberty (Italy) or Modernismo (Spain), the driving force behind it was everywhere the same—the determination to provide high-quality art products designed in accordance with avant-garde trends.

It still remained to find the means of realizing this aim, and here arose the all-important question of the materials to be employed. To begin with, no distinction was made between noble and less noble materials; in each case the most suitable material was chosen. The element best suited to achieve an elegant style, and best adapted to the structural necessities of metal materials, was line, and it was employed with a dual purpose ,being both decorative and constructive. "Line," wrote Van de Velde, "represents first of all the movement induced by inner activity"; so it also has a symbolic significance corresponding to the cultural climate of the period. It has been noted that Van de Velde was "the first architect to bear out the theories of *Einfühlung*" (Bruno Zevi). As a matter of fact, the line which was adopted (and not by Van de Velde alone) on account of its ability to emphasize symbolic implications tallied with the concept of "symbolic sympathy" as outlined by Robert Vischer in 1873 and formulated in the *Raumästhetik* of Theodor Lipps in 1897. The emphasis on line had behind it a long tradition which had been kept alive above all in English art from the time of Hogarth's "line of beauty"; and line of course had been the dominant stylistic feature of the Pre-Raphaelites and all the designers and illustrators who followed in their footsteps. Witness the book published by Walter Crane in 1900, *Line and Form*, in which line is considered not only as a pure decorative value but as an indication of movement, of dynamic rhythm. Like Van de Velde, Crane anticipated the idea of the "line of force" which appeared a few years later as a fundamental component of the dynamic symbolism of the Futurists, a symbolism with which the Secessionists undoubtedly had something in common.

England occupies a key position in the development of Art Nouveau. Students of the period, notably Pevsner, Tschudi Madsen and Schmutzler, have shown how much English artists contributed to the formation of the new style, not only on the ideological and theoretical plane (thanks of course to Ruskin and Morris) but also in the matter of design. "If the long sensitive curve, reminiscent of the lily's stem, an insect feeler, the filament of a blossom or occasionally a slender flame, the curve undulating, flowing and interplaying with others, sprouting from corners and covering asymmetrically all available surfaces, can be regarded as the leitmotiv of Art Nouveau," writes Nikolaus Pevsner, "then the first work of Art Nouveau which can be traced is Arthur H. Mackmurdo's cover of his book on Wren's City Churches published in 1883." This was ten years before Horta designed the Maison Tassel in Brussels, which is generally regarded as the first piece of architecture in the new style. The English artists moreover looked askance at developments on the continent, and Crane himself deplored the continental tendency towards excessive ornamentation. It is easy to see why he did so: the tradition of art for art's sake was very much alive on the continent, and many practitioners of Art Nouveau did no more than modernize, or aggravate, its purely decorative aspects; this went very much against the grain of those who had been schooled in the socialist ideals of the Arts and Crafts movement.

One of the most significant avant-garde movements of the nineties was launched in Glasgow; its commanding personality was the architect Charles Rennie Mackintosh, who with Herbert MacNair and the sisters Margaret and Frances Macdonald formed the group known as The Four. Mackintosh was not only an architect but a painter, decorator and illustrator. He and the other members of the Glasgow group were invited to show their work at an exhibition sponsored by L'Œuvre Artistique at Liège in 1895, at the Arts and Crafts Exhibition Society in London in 1896, and at the International Exhibition of Modern Decorative Art held in Turin in 1902. Mackintosh eludes any rigid classification; his work at times reveals inner contradictions and a certain eclecticism ranging from neo-Gothic to the Celtic Revival, but his fundamental concern was with the linear values of the composition. As a designer he aimed at the utmost clarity, preferring vertical rhythms to undulating lines with a view to bringing out to the full the structural properties of design. Space is organized in accordance with a rational pattern, almost geometrical in its transparency, and is modeled by the light glancing off the bright pure colors. His interior decorations are conceived in the same manner, with the same clarity and orderliness, and not as an accessory but as an integral part of the architectural space. Mackintosh was undoubtedly subject to symbolist influence, as evidenced by his imagery, but his sense of the stylistic unity of the artist's language, whatever the form of expression, is never equivocal or ambiguous. These principles are exemplified in his best work: the interior decorations for Miss Cranston's Tea Rooms, which he executed with George Walton in 1896-1897, and his designs for the Glasgow School of Art, built in 1897-1899, and remodeled and enlarged between 1907 and 1909.

Very different were the art ventures which, in the name of Art Nouveau, were taking place on the continent. They were confusing and contradictory ventures, so much so that it is not always easy to sift the good from the bad; for the most part in fact they belong more to social history than to art history. Alongside the work of the great architects and designers who appear today as the precursors of the modern movement, there came a fresh upsurge of academicism, a bewildering mixture of styles and ideologies, together with all the bric-a-brac of the so-called Decadents: this unleashed a riot of irrational forms in architecture and interior decoration which went far to counteract the genuine innovations of Horta, Van de Velde, Olbrich and Hoffmann. In themselves these tendencies are of little or no interest today. It is their effect that concerns us here; they deviated the logical course of events, marked a moment of cultural retrogression, and, instead of healing, only perpetuated the breach between art and public. Even today the picture remains confused. "This period," writes Luciano Benevolo, "while so close in time to contemporary life, is yet remote from us now. It is as if two world wars in the interval, besides smashing an incalculable number of homes furnished and decorated in the Art Nouveau style, had also broken all contact between ourselves and the men who designed those things." Even so, the forward-looking spirits, those who through Art Nouveau were able to break new ground, can at last be seen in something like historical perspective.

The house which in 1892-1893 Victor Horta designed and furnished, down to the last detail, for the engineer Tassel at 12 Rue de Turin in Brussels (now 6 Rue Paul Emile Janson), is regarded as the first architectural expression of the new style. All its elements, both architectural and decorative, are part and parcel of a single overall design; the coherence between structure and ornament is perfect; the interior space has the enfolding sweep of coiling lines; the materials are given a decorative elegance without ever being concealed, indeed they act as a compelling presence and radiate their linear dynamism. The Maison Tassel, together with the Hôtel Solvay (1895), the Hôtel Van Eetvelde (1895) and the artist's own house (1898), all in Brussels, are superb examples of private dwellings. But between 1896 and 1899 Horta ventured on something more exacting which demonstrated that the aesthetic of Art Nouveau did not apply only to the building of private residences but could meet the needs of society at large: this was the Maison du Peuple, designed as the headquarters of the Belgian Socialist Party and inaugurated by Jean Jaurès in 1900. "It is, among many others, an essential work," writes Robert L. Delevoy, "one of which it has been well said that it makes of Horta the Mies van der Rohe of Art Nouveau. Built on an unpromising piece of ground—sloping and shaped like a trapezium—it exploits all the resources of iron in order to give definition, without any intermediate supporting member, to the space of the meeting halls and the semi-transparent shell in glass and steel of a curved façade whose design was far in advance of its time."

If Horta was the poet of Art Nouveau architecture, Henry van de Velde was the most complex and many-sided artist of the movement, and the one most concerned with giving it an ideological foundation, a rationale. As an architect he has some very considerable achievements to his credit, from the Villa Bloemenwerf of 1895, at Uccle near Brussels, for

which he also designed the decorations and furnishings in their entirety, to the Kröller-Müller Museum at Otterlo, Holland, originally planned in 1933 but not completed till 1954 (Van de Velde's long and busy life only came to a close in 1957). The latter is one of his finest works, remarkable for the clarity of its layout and the perfect harmony between quality and function; it is a classic demonstration of the rational principles underlying Art Nouveau. Van de Velde applied his intellectual and artistic powers to the creation of new forms not only in architecture but also in interior decoration, furniture, wall hangings, tea and dinner sets in silver and porcelain, candelabra, bookbinding and page make-up. In doing so he gave fresh force and impetus, and a new sense of purpose, to the whole avant-garde movement. As a result, the design of an object became something more than a matter of abstract decorative beauty. A candelabrum, for example, or one of his famous kidney-shaped writing desks, are not free-standing objects isolated in the surrounding space, valid for their rhythmic forms and decorative presence alone; they are much more than that, they are part of a highly organized spatial unit, they are contributing elements suspending or stressing the movement of planes and masses. Above all they prove that the designer's every touch has an importance of its own and can contribute vitally to the intended effect.

In 1895 the German art dealer Samuel Bing paid a visit to Van de Velde, at Uccle, accompanied by the critic Julius Meier-Graefe, a keen student of the problems of modern art, author of some very discerning essays on the work of the French Impressionists, and founder of the German art magazine *Pan*. In Paris, the following year, Bing opened a shop called Maison de l'Art Nouveau where he displayed works by Van de Velde. Already active in France at that time were such designers and decorators as Gallé and Majorelle, and the new style developed fast in the years just before the Paris World's Fair of 1900, but in furnishings and objects rather than architecture. Yet in Paris itself a highly original architect as well as designer was then at work—Hector Guimard, who designed the Castel Béranger (1894-1898), the Humbert de Romans building (1902), and the Métro stations which gave rise in France to the ironic term "style métro." In Germany too the influence exerted by Van de Velde was very considerable. The artist himself moved to Berlin in 1900 and opened a studio there. He began teaching at the Weimar School of Applied Arts in 1904 and in 1907 took part in founding the Deutscher Werkbund at Munich, where he came in contact with architects like Peter Behrens who, following up the pioneer efforts of the great nineteenth-century designers, became the initiators of twentieth-century architecture in Europe.

Art Nouveau in Germany went by the name of Jugendstil, after the magazine *Jugend* launched in Munich in 1896, but the Deutscher Werkbund marked a decisive step beyond that early phase. The work of Peter Behrens, who contributed to *Jugend*, kept to the manner of Art Nouveau so long as his activities were limited to painting and decorating; but when he built his own house at Darmstadt in 1901 he broke away from it completely. Hermann Obrist, Otto Eckmann and August Endell, on the other hand, represent Jugendstil at its most typical, with all its limitations and purely decorative embellishments. Eckmann was a designer in a characteristically linear and floral style based on plant motifs and natural forms. Obrist, who founded an embroidery workshop first in Florence, then in Munich, drew on the same sources of inspiration, but in a less objective manner. In this he influenced Endell, who in 1897-1898 added to a Munich photographer's studio, the Atelier Elvira, a façade traversed by sweeping decorative rhythms, built up out of naturalistic elements. From Munich Jugendstil spread to Darmstadt where a whole colony of artists was at work under the patronage of the Grand Duke of Hesse, among them the Austrian architect Josef Maria Olbrich.

Vienna was one of the most important centers of the new style; it was also the place where the most decided reactions to it occurred. The Vienna Secession movement, bringing together vanguard artists and organizing exhibitions of their work, was founded in 1897 under the leadership of Olbrich and Gustav Klimt. But already before that Otto Wagner —under whom Olbrich studied—had given a new direction to Austrian architecture. Wagner was an architect who for a long time kept to the principles of classical symmetry; but after 1894, when he began teaching at the Vienna Academy, he ceased to imitate the traditional styles. He thought of the architect not as a specialist but as an artist, and it is this conception of his work, rather than his actual approach to problems of design, that links him up with the Belgian exponents of Art Nouveau. In these very years Wagner recast and renewed his style in the Stadtbahn stations which he built in Vienna between 1894 and 1897. Although they are proportioned on classical lines, their bold ornamentation goes beyond linear symbolism; indeed the use of sharply defined planes and the fine spareness of their design point the way to subsequent developments in architecture.

Like Wagner, Olbrich thought of the architect as being, first and foremost, the interpreter and elucidator of a particular artistic sensibility, and it was he who, in this spirit, built the exhibition hall of the Vienna Secession in 1898. The interior decoration was designed by Olbrich to reintroduce color into architecture, and his subsequent activity at Darmstadt, which came to an end with the Hochzeitsturm (1907) a year before his premature death, showed again how sensitive and resourceful he was in his handling of materials and techniques. His architecture goes beyond the style of the late nineteenth century, anticipating that of the twentieth. The same is true of Josef Hoffmann, another of Otto Wagner's pupils, who in 1903 opened a workshop of his own devoted to the applied arts, the Wiener Werkstätten, and designed a convalescent home at Purkersdorf. In 1904 Hoffmann began building one of the masterpieces of modern architecture, the Palais Stoclet in Brussels, brought to completion in 1914. His fusion of architecture and decoration, the converging influences of Van de Velde and Mackintosh which he so well assimilated, his ability to solve problems afresh and innovate successfully—all this placed him well to the fore in the international movement then being promoted by Art Nouveau. Yet he stands apart from it, in advance of it, in his rational organization of space, the interplay of planes, the attention he paid to the artistic value not of a superimposed decoration but of the materials themselves. Even the mosaic executed by Klimt inside the Palais Stoclet, despite its linear patterning and approximation to the symbolist aesthetic, reflects a sensibility and compositional design that no longer belong to the nineteenth century. Behrens in Germany, Olbrich, Hoffmann and above all Loos in Austria, together with Gaudi in Spain and Van de Velde himself (but not Horta), were already working in the spirit of the twentieth century.

ARCHITECTURE AND DECORATION

Art Nouveau set out to give a style *to all the things that surround men in daily life. The great architects of the late nineteenth century resolved the conflict between architecture and technics in the most logical manner—that is, by integrating decoration with structure. Horta, in Brussels, set an example with his Maison Tassel of 1892-1893, and again, a few years later, with the Hôtel Van Eetvelde and the Hôtel Solvay. In accordance with the Art Nouveau aesthetic, line was the fundamental component of Horta's compositional syntax, and by means of line he restored their expressive value to structures which were at once functional and decorative. Into the space thus created were inserted furnishings, doors, windows and railings designed in the same style. Such was also the case with Guimard and above all with Mackintosh, whose mural decorations and furniture, even though external to the structures housing them, have the same vertical rhythm which characterizes the distribution of space and volumes.*

Mackintosh exerted a certain influence on the artists of the Vienna Secession, and very probably on Gustav Klimt, whose paintings were conceived in relation to an architecture whose forms must have been based on more or less the same principles. This is true not only of his decorations—and the decorations Klimt made for Hoffmann's Palais Stoclet in Brussels undoubtedly number among his masterpieces—but also of his easel pictures. For his paintings were always designed to harmonize with the room in which they were to hang, or which they were to decorate; this was the very reverse of the method adopted by Whistler who, in the case of the Peacock Room and his Princess of the Land of Porcelain, *adapted the room to the picture. With Klimt the simplification of forms, the arbitrary but intensely expressive concision of line and the flat, two-dimensional space are in perfect keeping with the intended purpose of the picture; so too is its elaborate textural richness, as sumptuous as a mosaic, with a spirited play of surface accents.*

Louis Sullivan, one of the great nineteenth-century pioneers of modern architecture, could not but concern himself with the problem of decoration, even though his own conceptions, those of the functionalism of the Chicago School, tended to exclude decoration. "Ornament," wrote Sullivan, "should appear not as something receiving the spirit of the structure, but as a thing expressing that spirit by virtue of differential growth." Ornament and structure, then, can find their appropriate synthesis only through a process of elaboration over which presides a single unified conception. The decorative element is a necessary component of architecture, not a mere accessory.

HECTOR GUIMARD (1867-1942). ENTRANCE OF THE CASTEL BÉRANGER, PARIS, 1894-1898.

VICTOR HORTA (1861-1947). STAIRCASE IN THE HOTEL SOLVAY, BRUSSELS, 1895-1900.

CHARLES RENNIE MACKINTOSH (1868-1928). PRELIMINARY DESIGN FOR MURAL DECORATION OF MISS CRANSTON'S BUCHANAN STREET
TEA ROOMS, GLASGOW (DETAIL), 1896-1897. WATERCOLOR. UNIVERSITY OF GLASGOW ART COLLECTIONS.

GUSTAV KLIMT (1862-1918). THE THREE AGES OF WOMAN, 1908. GALLERIA NAZIONALE D'ARTE MODERNA, ROME.

LOUIS SULLIVAN (1856-1924). DETAIL OF THE STAIRWAY IN THE AUDITORIUM BUILDING, CHICAGO, 1886-1890. PRESENT STATE. BY PERMISSION OF ROOSEVELT UNIVERSITY, CHICAGO.

life. The leading European architects of the late nineteenth century, men like Van de Velde, Horta, Olbrich, Behrens, and also Berlage, never let the decorative element get out of hand. Their work is a recapitulation of the theories and practice of all those who had preceded them in the great task of renewing and modernizing architecture. They took to heart the lessons not only of Ruskin and Morris but of Viollet-le-Duc and the engineers who had put metal structures to the service of modern communications. Horta's Maison du Peuple in Brussels offers a variety of perspectives turning on an incurved façade which brings out the tension of the dynamic rhythms inherent in the very structure of the metal supporting spans. The auditorium inside, located on the top floor instead of the ground floor, as was usually the case, is remarkable for its rational organization of space, punctuated by the exposed metal supports rising gracefully from the floor to the roof. In complete contrast to this restraint are the exuberant decorative and floral patterns of the inner staircase in Endell's Atelier Elvira in Munich. Here we have two different aspects of Art Nouveau: on the one hand, a decorative felicity integrated into the structure, permeating it without debasing it; on the other, an excess of ornament masking the constructive function of the metallic element.

A renewal can be brought about in more ways than one. While Horta and Van de Velde achieved their aims by way of Symbolism, then very much alive in Brussels, Otto Wagner in Vienna achieved his by way of a plastic vision which unified the relations between masses and surfaces. The resulting transformations were equally effective, leading to the creation of a new style in which the logical clarity of the compositional order was untroubled by extraneous elements. Berlage in Holland achieved a similar clarity of design on the basis of Gothic and Romanesque forms. His rationalism seems to

HENRY VAN DE VELDE (1863-1957). VILLA BLOEMENWERF AT UCCLE, BRUSSELS, 1895.

AUGUST ENDELL (1871-1925). INNER STAIRCASE
IN THE ATELIER ELVIRA, MUNICH, 1897-1898.

VICTOR HORTA (1861-1947).
STAIRS OF THE MAISON TASSEL, BRUSSELS, 1892-189

VICTOR HORTA (1861-1947). AUDITORIUM IN THE MAISON DU PEUPLE, BRUSSELS, 1896-1899.

OTTO WAGNER (1841-1918).
ENTRANCE OF THE STADTBAHN STATION IN THE KARLSPLATZ, VIENNA, 1897.

6

TOWARDS A NEW ARCHITECTURE

In 1895, when he was only thirty-two, Henry van de Velde built a house of his own, the Villa Bloemenwerf, at Uccle, near Brussels. It represents a landmark in his career, much as the Red House does in the career of William Morris. Thirty years later he spoke of it as an experience which, by opening his eyes to the full meaning of human dignity, had clinched his determination to change the face of the world. For us it is an example of how an architect, starting from the symbolist premises of Art Nouveau, could work out a genuinely architectonic design, in no way irrational, based on a logical distribution of rooms and space, with a perfect balance between formal intuition and technical realization. Bloemenwerf is a house which, as Van de Velde himself emphasized, developed from the floor plan and inner core outwards, not from the façade inwards. Though without any symmetry of a classical order, it yet has a harmony of its own, achieved through the organic layout of the rooms. It was a house of a new kind, wholly modern in conception, which in some ways anticipated the rational solutions of twentieth-century architecture.

Van de Velde showed that Art Nouveau, when not wholly given over to mere decoration, when not subordinating the technician to the decorator, could contribute vitally to the development of an organic style of design adapted to the conditions of modern

HENDRIK PETRUS BERLAGE (1856-1934). THE STOCK EXCHANGE AT AMSTERDAM, 1899-1903.

JOSEF MARIA OLBRICH (1867-1908).
THE ARTIST'S HOUSE
AT DARMSTADT, 1901.

PETER BEHRENS (1868-1940).
INTERIOR OF THE ARTIST'S HOUSE
AT DARMSTADT, 1901.

186

derive directly from that of Viollet-le-Duc, but in actual practice, as in the Amsterdam Stock Exchange which he built between 1899 and 1903, Berlage made a notable advance. Decoration is provided solely by the natural texture and colors of the materials composing the structure, colors and texture varying with the quality of the light. The chromatic values thus obtained remain subdued and restful, their rhythm governed by the openings and volumes of the building. Traditional forms, treated with so rational a simplicity, thus become the vehicle of a wholly modern sensibility.

In the work of Wagner's best pupil, Josef Maria Olbrich, the limitations of decorative symbolism were likewise overcome by a firm grasp of architectonic values. Olbrich too obtained his decorative effects by bringing out the chromatic values of architecture, but this did not prevent him from achieving a rational organization of volumes and keeping a strict eye on the quality of the decoration. This is particularly true of the house which he built for himself at Darmstadt in 1901; its compact geometry remains undisturbed by the colored decorative elements which go to diversify its outer surfaces. By the time he died in 1908, at the age of only forty-one, Olbrich had gone well beyond Art Nouveau. To transcend Art Nouveau did not however mean to repudiate its lesson, especially when that lesson, embodying Morris's teaching, indicated that the problem of house design and that of interior decoration were inseparable and had to be solved together. Van de Velde in 1895 designed all the furnishings for Bloemenwerf, and in 1901 Behrens did the same for his house at Darmstadt. This conception of an overall unity of design reached its full maturity when Behrens, after joining the Deutscher Werkbund, was commissioned by the A.E.G., an electrical company in Berlin, not only to build its plant but to design its products.

MODERN STRUCTURES

Modern art, as Theodor W. Adorno shrewdly observes, has brought to the surface everything that most of us would like to forget. This explains the bourgeois distaste for the modern movements; it explains society's repeated attempts to gag the artist, to set limits to his activities, to dismiss them as being only of marginal interest with no bearing on the important issues of life. Art Nouveau arose at the end of the nineteenth century in reaction against those attempts, but in so far as it remained within the limits of decorative art it brought a solution no nearer; indeed it ended up by pandering to the tastes of an ever wider public. Hence the success it enjoyed; hence its widespread diffusion as part of a culture for the masses, beyond the sphere of art, into the world of dress and fashion, into that category of the superficial and external which the Germans designate as *Kitsch*. These were serious limitations, and because of them Art Nouveau was speedily forgotten (except of course for the work of a few leading personalities); because of them it failed to enter permanently into the stylistic vocabulary of our century. By the end of the nineteenth century art was no longer intended to flatter or edify; a picture, a piece of sculpture, a building, had ceased to be a grandiloquent monument or an object of contemplation. Each was a reworking of reality whereby the artist claimed not only his place but his function in a society which he hoped to remold nearer to his heart's desire.

The masses moreover considered the results of scientific research much as they considered those of art. Unconcerned with the methods employed and even less with the meaning of the structures those methods served to define, they did not inquire into the reasons behind them but accepted them as a revealed, ineluctable truth; they renounced their own critical faculties and submitted to an élite. In the same way the public looked to artists for a revelation, in fact an abstract revelation, for they demanded landscapes and figures conforming to preconceived,

altogether conventional ideas, confusing truth with the semblance of truth. Artists proceeded to give them the very reverse, producing images for which they had no authority; and in a few years' time, inferring all possible consequences from the line of development marked out by the masters of the nineteenth century, artists were no longer painting landscapes and figures at all, no longer devising delicate harmonies of color: now they painted squares and rectangles, and violent contrasts of color. Now, too, architects refused to indulge any more in decorative fantasies, and the dwelling house became a *machine à habiter*. Art had in fact become a touchstone, a mirror held up to things as they are, to the realities of the human condition. Art was thus placed in a position to render men a service, to provide them, thanks to the autonomy of its values, with instruments of knowledge, above all of self-knowledge.

All this began in the second half of the nineteenth century; between 1870 and 1880 the Impressionists initiated this process of transformation. Cézanne, Monet, Gauguin and Van Gogh, one after the other, pressed the process to its ultimate conclusions, each starting from much the same premises but each going his own way. Impressionism marks the point of departure of all modern art. It says much for the power of stimulation behind that original impetus that it should have been carried forward and elaborated on both by painters like Monet and Cézanne, who had themselves contributed to form the impressionist way of seeing, and by others like Van Gogh and Gauguin, who had taken it up and carefully weighed its possibilities. If art in the hands of these men could no longer be equated with contemplation, neither could it be based on sensations alone as discerned and ordered by the conscious mind in its sifting of the data of visual perception. It fell to Cézanne to restore to the intellectual faculties their rightful place in the artistic process. What he called *la petite sensation* was the starting point of a process whereby the notions born of nature return to the bosom of nature. "Cézanne," wrote Merleau-Ponty, "never set out to 'paint like a brute,' but to bring our understanding, our ideas, the sciences, perspective and tradition again into contact with the natural world which they are meant to comprehend, to bring face to face with nature, as he said, the sciences which derive from nature."

Cézanne restored all its logic to the process of ordering sensations, a process which is not intuitive. If linear perspective went by the board, together with the conventional cube-shaped picture space, this was in order to intensify the emotional power of the result, to pour into this many-faceted space a greater volume of emotive sensations; it was also and above all to restore to the representation a logical order deriving from an empirical, experimental consideration of the process of organizing sensations. This experimentation was conducted so slowly, so painstakingly, that Zola was prompted to dismiss Cézanne as a failure, a *génie avorté*; it was in fact a process of investigation that Cézanne was engaged in, one running parallel to that of science which, by that time, had outgrown the dogmatism of the Positivists and was moving towards the theory of relativity. Coming at the end of the long, troubled line of development of nineteenth-century art, Cézanne was the artist of genius who, himself deeply troubled and often unsure of himself, opened the age of indetermination, an age more vital and stimulating than the epoch of dogmatic assurance which preceded it.

Monet's approach to form and composition was altogether different. To an order reconstructed on the basis of conscious experience, Monet seemed intent on opposing the disorder of indiscriminate perception; to a patterned sequence of volumes in recession, the decorative synthesis of light reflected on the picture surface; to the regular, full-bodied plasticity of a geometric order, the extension of a form which no longer has any limits. On the other hand, Monet's aims and motives were much the same as Cézanne's. Both attributed a determinant value to the act of painting itself, and saw the creative act as conferring an order, a certain order, on perception; for both it was always in the dimension of the conscious mind that occurred the critical selection not only of the phenomenon but of the actual procedure to be followed. It is commonly

supposed that Monet produced his finest work in his impressionist period, in the 1870s, that the quality of his later paintings suffered from an over-emphasis on the analysis of light effects to the detriment of formal synthesis. Undoubtedly there was a time in Monet's career when he did perhaps concentrate too exclusively on light analysis, but the paintings of the last thirty years of his life were far in advance of their time, so far that their significance is only now being realized.

While Cézanne inquired into the function of the image, Monet investigated its organic structure. A picture by Monet is an object which extends beyond itself, it is no longer limited by the four edges of the canvas, but envelopes the beholder and sweeps him up in its pulsation. While Cézanne restored to painting its intellectual attributes, Monet gave it an increased vitality through the integration of image and matter—image and not form, concreteness that is, and not symbol. The picture sprang to life as an act of existence, and it is not by chance that the full significance of Monet's last works has only been grasped in recent years in the light of the informal aesthetic of post-war painting. Monet was a painter who never forgot that he was such even in the most tragic moments of his life. It is recorded of him that even at the deathbed of one very dear to him the artist found himself involuntarily observing, with a painter's eye, the changes of color that came over the dying person's face. For Monet, who reduced everything to painting, the synthesis was no longer only a matter of the structural organization of the elements of vision, it was a synthesis of acts, of past and present, of memory. Seen in the perspective of history, only a few years intervened between David and Monet, but that short space of time witnessed a momentous change in the ideological significance and content of the work of art.

The work of Gauguin and Van Gogh, though they approached the problem from another angle, pointed the same way. Both showed clearly that, for the artist, there was no more satisfaction to be drawn from the contemplation of the world as it is; they were conscious, Van Gogh above all, of the impossibility of evangelizing men who had departed so far from their real selves. For Gauguin the symbol is an image, it has a value in its own right and not as an allegory; allegory would give the formal equivalent of an idea, as in Puvis de Chavannes but not in Gauguin. The world of perception is dominated by the world of consciousness, and the two-dimensional space of the composition restores to painting the immediate significance of the message which painting conveys; that two-dimensional space enables direct communication. Art thus became more human: refusing to render nature as organized arbitrarily in terms of conventional representation, and substituting another type of arbitrary representation, Gauguin proposed the image of a complex existence expressed in all its components, including both what man knows and what he would prefer not to know.

Gauguin's execution, which was subordinated to the emotive sensation, was quite as normative and intellectual as Cézanne's. The myth of the savage, the primitive, was no picturesque or romantic myth, no equivalent of a Gospel parable of purity and poverty through which salvation could be attained. Gauguin and Cézanne left the parables to Emile Bernard—"Emilio Bernardinos, noblest of aesthetes," as Cézanne mockingly called him. Painting had abandoned the Empyrean and come down among the sinners, as into a circle of the damned beyond hope, not to convert but to observe and record. Van Gogh transformed painting into a cry of despair transcending problems of form, and by doing so transformed his own existence. First by an organization of the brushwork and space, next by the destruction of logical order of any kind, he found his way back to the different, arbitrary order created by the successive acts of existence; he unsealed within himself, in the face of death, the deepest sources of pity for the human condition. What is man's destiny? "Whence come we, what are we, whither go we?" asked Gauguin. For him there was a ray of hope; it lay in investigating the possibilities of knowledge inherent in the pictorial process. Van Gogh had no time for that; he at once

expressed in painting his state of mind and spirit, harassed as he was by questionings for which there seemed to be no answers. The result was a different synthesis, behind which lurked the shadow of death as a term of comparison for life and for the work of art itself. To his dramatic questioning the answer seemed to be negative: destiny is ambiguous, the position of art indeterminate. Form and compositional rhythm remained perturbed, remained open, and coloring was remote from the local colors of nature; the data of perception were no longer sufficient to appease anxiety of mind.

But who any longer sought security? Not Cézanne, a prey to doubt; not Monet, who was overthrowing the inner structures of matter; not Gauguin, who turned away from subdued harmonies to jarring contrasts of pure colors laid in side by side; not Van Gogh, for whom the only imminent certainty was death. With these men we are far away from the controlled anxiety of the Impressionists. And yet Impressionism had borne fruit, it had reminded the artist of his responsibilities as a man, it had created a dimension, that of the conscious mind, which painting had never known before. It opened for artists the doors to a world teeming with questions which they could not be expected to settle once and for all, but which were always a fruitful source of expression, of doubt, of despair—in short, a vital source of thought and ever-renewed endeavor. Art had come down from the altars and out of the palaces, to mingle with all men and share in their trials and perplexities. It no longer looked back to the past but forward to the future, intensely conscious of the inevitable vicissitudes which lay ahead and through which there could not be an easy path to grace and salvation. Everything now turned on man, on the thought and action by which alone he could hope to redeem the precariousness of the human condition.

PAUL GAUGUIN (1848-1903). HINA TE FATOU: THE MOON AND THE EARTH, 1893.
COLLECTION THE MUSEUM OF MODERN ART, NEW YORK, LILLIE P. BLISS COLLECTION.

GAUGUIN - CÉZANNE - VAN GOGH - MONET

Gauguin painted Hina Te Fatou *in Tahiti in 1893. Hina is the moon goddess, who gives life to all that appertains to her; Te Fatou is the earth god who condemns everything to pass away, even man and all that has nourished him. The myth of all-devouring night is as old as the world but particularly appeals to the modern artist who seeks in it an explanation, or at the least a justification, of his own destiny. But for the painter the sole reality is painting, which takes up the myth and transforms it into an image, thus releasing it from contingencies of time and place which would only devitalize it. For Cézanne, too, artistic creation is the only means of attaining to truth. All the light intensity which Impressionism had opened his eyes to, was now put to the service of a representation which no longer had anything in common with traditional modes of painting. A synthesis was achieved in depth between light and pictorial mass, and the picture space, emotive rather than descriptive, concentrates in itself the successive moments of consciousness, merging them into a new time dimension.*

The rocks of the Bibémus quarry as painted by Cézanne are not so very different from those of the quarry painted by Van Gogh in 1889, while undergoing treatment in the asylum of Saint-Rémy. But there is a vehemence in Van Gogh's rocks that is lacking in Cézanne's. Van Gogh's colors, too, are colors of the mind, but his aggressive recasting of natural data is wholly sensuous. Where Cézanne recognizes the impossibility of a representation in known terms, Van Gogh bridles up at it. His attitude to nature is the reverse of Cézanne's: for Van Gogh a rock or a cornfield can become a cosmic tragedy; every pebble, every leaf, every ear of corn is swept with a gust of tragic emotion, the reflection of his own tormented spirit.

Ten years later, in the garden of his house at Giverny, Monet began painting his waterscapes—a placid pond, overspread with waterlilies, in a lush setting of trees and flowers. Here too, though with none of Van Gogh's passionate vehemence, nature is transformed, perspective done away with, colors intensified not only in their constituent pigments but in their tonal relationships. Everything is melted down in glowing light; even the texture of the paints is thinner than in earlier works, the Rouen Cathedral *series for example. There is no concession here to the merely picturesque and the work is in fact a magisterial piece of decorative art. Monet's style in the last years of his life is certainly no less modern than that of the Fauves and Cubists.*

PAUL CÉZANNE (1839-1906). ROCKS AT BIBÉMUS, 1898-1900. FOLKWANG MUSEUM, ESSEN.

VINCENT VAN GOGH (1853-1890). THE FONTETTES RAVINE, 1889. KRÖLLER-MÜLLER MUSEUM, OTTERLO, HOLLAND.

VINCENT VAN GOGH (1853-1890). EARS OF WHEAT, 1890. COLLECTION IR. V.W. VAN GOGH, STEDELIJK MUSEUM, AMSTERDAM.

CLAUDE MONET (1840-1926). THE WATER GARDEN AT GIVERNY. MUSÉE DE PEINTURE ET SCULPTURE, GRENOBLE.

A MAN

The self-portrait painted by Van Gogh in the asylum at Saint-Rémy, to which he had asked to be admitted for treatment barely a year before his death, is that of a man ready to make whatever sacrifice may be required of him. The face is treated without any hint of self-pity, and this is true not only of the actual features but above all of the psychological characterization. Here is no wavering or indecision but a courageous firmness and sincerity. The gaunt, emaciated features, brought alive with quick, excited strokes of the brush, are like a summing-up of his tragic life-story; they tell of his lust for life and, at the same time, of his fatal incapacity to bear the stresses of a life so intensely lived. He was the victim of a mental unrest continually sharpened by an inability to come to terms with the realities of ordinary life. Where he hoped for serenity he found vexation of spirit, and painting gave him no release. He felt an irresistible urge to communicate with others: it drove him to renounce his mission among the miners and peasants of the North, to abandon Paris and the easy path opened up to him by the revelation of Impressionism and Post-Impressionism, to immerse himself in the sun of Provence, to give up preaching for painting, contemplation for participation.

But where does this ultimately lead to? It led, in the event, to the loss of reason in dramatic circumstances. The experience of the senses fails to justify a way of life when the world, taken as a whole, is seen or divined in all its extra-sensory complexity. The only solution would be to interrelate all things, to embody them all in painting, in a new order; but that is impossible, and even the mental effort to create a style is dominated by emotions that well up from the depths of an unquiet mind. Van Gogh came up against reality as against a barrier: "Instead of trying to render exactly what I see before me, I use color more arbitrarily in order to express myself strongly." Painting and life became one, and just as his troubled, anxiety-ridden soul led him to destroy himself, so he also destroyed every pre-existing pictorial structure. It was Van Gogh who introduced into modern art that sense of insecurity which is so closely connected with the human condition, and from which, since that time, it has been impossible to escape.

VINCENT VAN GOGH (1853–1890). SELF-PORTRAIT WITH PALETTE, 1889. BY COURTESY OF MR AND MRS JOHN HAY WHITNEY, NEW YORK.

INDEX OF NAMES
LIST OF ILLUSTRATIONS

INDEX OF NAMES

FRANCASTEL Pierre 23, 27, 68, 69, 77, 100, 115.
FRY Roger (1866-1934) 135.
FURNESS Frank 89.

GACHET Dr Paul (1828-1909) 45.
GALLÉ Emile (1846-1904) 29, 31, 146, 163, 166, 169, 173.
GAMBETTA Léon (1838-1882) 12.
GARNIER Charles (1825-1898) 30.
GARNIER Tony (1869-1948) 66, 67, 69.
GASQUET Joachim (1873-1921) 120, 131.
GAUDI Antoni (1852-1926) 174.
GAUGUIN Paul (1848-1903) 29, 45, 99, 115, 122, 123, 146/148, 157, 158, 171, 189/193.
GAUTIER Théophile (1811-1872) 10, 11.
GÉROME Jean-Léon (1824-1904) 102.
GIEDION Siegfried 10, 21, 27, 41, 85, 87, 91.
GIFFARD Henry Jacques (1825-1882) 30.
GIORGIONE (1476/77-1510) 101.
GIRAULT Charles-Louis (1851-?) 30.
GLEYRE Marc-Charles (1807-1876) 100, 102.
GODIN Jean-Baptiste (1817-1888) 65.
GOETHE Johann Wolfgang (1749-1832) 10, 11.
GOMBRICH Ernst H. 135.
GONCOURT Edmond (1822-1896) 39, 42.
GONCOURT Jules (1830-1870) 39, 42.
GOODWIN Arthur C. (1866-1929) 86.
GOUNOD Charles (1818-1893) 39.
GOYA Francisco de (1746-1828) 44.
GRACE John 27.
GREENOUGH Horatio (1805-1852) 11, 23, 87, 88.
GROPIUS Walter (1883) 171.
GUADET Julien (1834-1908) 70.
GUARINI Guarino (1624-1683) 68.
GUIMARD Hector (1867-1942) 115, 173, 176.

HALÉVY Daniel (1872-?) 12.
HARDMAN John 27.
HARDY Léopold Amédée (1829-1894) 39.
HASSAM Childe (1859-1935) 86.
HAUSSMANN Eugène, Baron (1809-1891) 11, 63/66, 99, 100.
HAWTHORNE Nathaniel (1804-1864) 63, 65, 86, 87.
HELMHOLTZ Ferdinand von (1821-1894) 121.
HENNEBIQUE François (1842-1921) 70, 72.
HERRIOT Edouard (1872-1957) 67.
HEWITT George Wattson (1842-1916) 89.
HODLER Ferdinand (1853-1918) 99, 149, 151.
HOFFMANN Josef (1870-1955) 31, 172, 174, 175.
HOGARTH William (1697-1764) 171.
HOLABIRD William (1854-1923) 88, 89.
HOMER Winslow (1836-1910) 104, 105.
HOREAU Hector (1801-1872) 33.
HORTA Victor (1861-1947) 31, 122, 146, 167, 172/175, 177, 182/184.
HOSCHEDÉ Ernest 45.
HOWARD Ebenezer (1850-1928) 64/67.
HUGHES John (1677-1720) 70.
HUGO Victor (1802-1885) 21.
HUNT William Holman (1827-1910) 136.
HUNT William Morris (1824-1879) 86.
HURD Richard (1720-1808) 70.
HUSSERL Edmund (1859-1938) 31.

IBELS Henri-Gabriel (1867-1936) 148.
INGRES Jean-Dominique (1780-1867) 11, 28, 29, 59, 102, 123, 145, 147.
INNESS George (1825-1894) 86.
ISABEY Félix (1821-1895) 28.

JAURÈS Jean (1859-1914) 173.
JECKYLL Thomas 139.
JEFFERSON Thomas (1743-1826) 11, 86.
JENNEY William Le Baron (1832-1907) 70, 88, 89, 94, 97.
JONES Owen (1809-1874) 27, 34, 137.
JONGKIND Johann Barthold (1819-1891) 47, 50, 99.

KLEE Paul (1879-1940) 169.
KLIMT Gustav (1862-1918) 174, 175, 179.
KOECHLIN 39.
KRANTZ Jean-Baptiste-Sébastien (1817-1899) 29, 34.
KREBS 30.
KRUPP Alfred (1812-1887) 64.

LABORDE Léon, Count (1807-1869) 26, 77, 85.
LABROUSTE Henri (1801-1875) 11, 23, 28, 69, 72, 74, 87.
LACOMBE Georges (1868-1916) 148.
LAFORGUE Jules (1860-1887) 106.
LATROBE Benjamin Henry (1764-1820) 86.
LAUTREC Henri de TOULOUSE- (1864-1901) 122, 123, 125, 130, 147, 148.
LAVAL Charles 29.
LAWSON Ernest (1873-1939) 86.
L'ENFANT Pierre Charles (1755-1825) 11, 86.
LETHABY William Richard (1857-1931) 138.
LEVER William Hesketh (1851-1925) 66.
LEYLAND Frederick R. 139.
LIEBERMANN Max (1847-1935) 45.
LIPPS Theodor (1851-1914) 171.
LOOS Adolf (1870-1933) 174.
LOUVET Louis-Albert (1860-?) 30.
LUCE Maximilien (1858-1941) 121.

MACDONALD Frances (1874-1921) 172.
MACDONALD Margaret (1865-1933) 172.
MACKINTOSH Charles Rennie (1868-1928) 31, 146, 164, 168, 172, 174, 175, 178.
MACKMURDO Arthur Heygate (1851-1942) 138, 164, 165, 172.
MAC-MAHON Marshal (1808-1893) 101.
MACNAIR Herbert J. 172.
MAETERLINCK Maurice (1862-1949) 169.
MAILLOL Aristide (1861-1944) 148.
MAJORELLE Louis (1859-1926) 173.
MANET Edouard (1832-1883) 11/13, 16, 19/21, 28, 29, 42/45, 99/102, 106, 110, 120, 145, 147.
MARCONI Guglielmo (1874-1937) 10.
MARX Karl (1818-1883) 9, 22, 63, 65.
MARX Roger 29, 30.
MATISSE Henri (1869-1954) 145, 146.
MATTHIESSEN F. O. 87.
MAUPASSANT Guy de (1850-1893) 39.
MAXWELL James Clerk (1831-1879) 121, 123.
MEIER-GRAEFE Julius 173.
MEISSONIER Ernest (1815-1891) 39.
MELVILLE Herman (1819-1891) 86.
MERLEAU-PONTY Maurice (1908-1961) 100, 190.
METCALF Willard L. (1858-1925) 86.
MIES VAN DER ROHE Ludwig (1886) 173.

MILLAIS Sir John Everett (1829-1896) 45, 136.
MILLET Jean-François (1814-1875) 13, 14, 29, 42, 45, 101.
MINTON Herbert 27.
MONDRIAN Piet (1872-1944) 122.
MONET Claude (1840-1926) 12, 29, 45, 47, 49, 99/101, 106, 111, 114, 120, 122, 123, 145, 189/190, 193, 197.
MONFREID Daniel de (1856-1929) 29.
MONSELET Charles (1825-1888) 44.
MOORE George (1852-1933) 135.
MORÉAS Jean (1856-1910) 145, 147.
MOREAU Gustave (1826-1898) 45, 145, 146, 148, 149, 153.
MOROT Aimé-Nicolas (1850-1913) 45.
MORRIS William (1834-1896) 10/12, 22, 23, 25, 26, 28, 30, 31, 43, 44, 63, 66, 70, 87, 135/141, 163, 164, 169, 171, 172, 181, 182, 187.
MULLER Charles-Louis (1815-1892) 28.
MUMFORD Lewis 23, 63.
MUNCH Edvard (1863-1944) 45, 99, 149, 155.
MUYBRIDGE Eadweard (1830-1904) 58, 59.
MYERS George 27.

NADAR, Gaspard-Félix TOURNACHON (1820-1910) 45, 56, 59.
NAPOLEON III (1808-1873) 13, 20, 43, 44, 64.
NASH John (1752-1835) 71.
NEUFCHÂTEAU François de 26.
NEWMAN John Henry (1801-1890) 136.
NIEUWERKERKE Alfred Emilien (1811-1892), Count 12, 20, 28, 43.
NOUGIER 39.

OBRIST Hermann (1863-1927) 174.
OLBRICH Josef Maria (1867-1908) 172, 174, 182, 186, 187.
ORTEGA Y GASSET José (1883-1955) 10.
OVERBECK Friedrich (1789-1869) 42.
OWEN Robert (1771-1858) 64, 65.

PAGE William (1811-1885) 86.
PALLADIO Andrea (1508-1580) 86.
PARKER Barry 67.
PAXTON Sir Joseph (1803-1865) 26, 27, 33/35, 42, 70, 71, 78, 85, 101.
PETIT Georges 29.
PEVSNER Nikolaus 27, 99, 138, 172.
PICA Vittorio 45.
PICARD Alfred 30.
PICASSO Pablo (1881) 146.
PIOT René (1868-1934) 148.
PISSARRO Camille (1830-1903) 12, 29, 43, 45, 99/101, 106, 109, 120, 123.
PIUS IX, Pope (1846-1878) 9.
PLUMET Charles (1861-1928) 30.
POLLOCK Jackson (1912-1956) 149.
PROUDHON Pierre-Joseph (1809-1865) 11, 22, 63.
PROUST Antonin (1832-1905) 29, 102.
PRUD'HON Pierre-Paul (1758-1823) 29.
PUGIN Augustus Welby (1812-1852) 22, 27, 70.
PUVIS DE CHAVANNES Pierre (1824-1898) 29, 45, 46, 145, 146, 148/150, 190.

RAIMONDI Marcantonio (about 1480-about 1534) 101.
RANSON Paul (1864-1909) 148, 157.
RAPHAEL (1483-1520) 123, 136.
REDGRAVE Richard 27.

LIST OF ILLUSTRATIONS

PRINTED ON THE PRESSES OF
ÉDITIONS D'ART ALBERT SKIRA
15 NOVEMBER 1965

PHOTOGRAPHS BY

Alpenland, Vienna (page 184 bottom), Maurice Babey, Basel (pages 75, 110, 112, 150 bottom, 155), Berger Photographs, Glasgow (page 50 top), Henry B. Beville, Alexandria, Va. (pages 16, 51, 107, 124, 126 bottom, 144), Paul Boissonnas, Geneva (page 165 bottom right), Lee Boltin, New York (pages 114, 118, 152), Bulloz, Paris (page 35 bottom, 79 top), Chevojon Frères, Paris (pages 36 top and bottom, 38 bottom, 81), Chicago Architectural Photographing Company (pages 37 bottom, 93, 94, 95, 96, 180), R. Cowper, Glasgow (page 178), John R. Freeman & Co., Ltd, London (pages 129, 140, 141, 142, 143), George Eastman House, Rochester, N.Y. (pages 55 top and bottom, 56, 57, 58 bottom), J.J. de Goede, Amsterdam (page 195), Graphic-Photo, Paris (pages 8, 14, 50 bottom, 74, 117, 153, 156, 176), Sherwin Greenberg Studio Inc., Buffalo, N.Y. (page 104 top), Carlfred Halbach, Ratingen (page 194), Martin Hesse, Bern (page 151), Léo Hilber, Fribourg (page 154), A. F. Kersting, London (page 73), H. Kessels, Brussels (page 183 top), Raymond Laniepce, Paris (pages 19, 109, 113, 116, 126 top, 127, 158, 160), Frank Lerner, New York (pages 192, 199), Louis Loose, Brussels (pages 130, 177 bottom right), Eli Lotar, Paris (jacket and page 80), La Photothèque, Paris (pages 18, 131), Umberto Rossi, Venice (page 104 bottom), Jean Roubier, Paris (pages 79-80 bottom), Oscar Savio, Rome (pages 37-38 top, 119, 179), Schmölz-Huth, Cologne-Marienburg (page 48), H. Stebler, Bern (page 55 top), Dr Franz Stoedtner, Düsseldorf (pages 183 bottom left, 185), and the photographic departments of the following museums: Amsterdam, Rijksmuseum (page 165 top right), Amsterdam, Stedelijk Museum (pages 49 top, 196), Cambridge, Mass., Fogg Art Museum, Harvard University (page 15), Cleveland Museum of Art (page 150 top), Darmstadt, Hessisches Landesmuseum (page 186 top and bottom), London, Victoria and Albert Museum (pages 35 top, 166 bottom right), New York, Museum of Modern Art (pages 58 top, 161), Trondheim, Nordenfjeldske Kunstindustrimuseum (page 166 bottom left), Zurich, Kunstgewerbemuseum (page 166 top left and right). Other photographs by courtesy of the Ministère des Travaux Publics, Brussels (page 184 top), Conzett & Huber, Zurich (pages 49 bottom, 111, 197), Gerd Hatje, Verleger, Stuttgart-Bad Cannstatt (pages 168 bottom, 183 bottom right), Baroness V. Horta, Brussels (page 167) and Fabriques de Chocolat Menier, Paris (page 79 bottom).

COLOR PLATES ENGRAVED BY GUÉZELLE & RENOUARD, PARIS

COVER PLATE ENGRAVED BY ACTUAL, BIENNE (SWITZERLAND)

BLACK AND WHITE PLATES BY IMPRIMERIES RÉUNIES, LAUSANNE

PRINTED IN SWITZERLAND